THE EDITORS

Prof Hermann Giliomee is currently head of the Department of Political Studies at the University of Cape Town. He is an historian by training and the author of several books in the fields of South African history and political trends and issues, including *Ethnic power mobilised: can South Africa change?* (with Heribert Adam, Yale University Press); *Up against the fences* (with Lawrence Schlemmer, St Martins Press); and *Afrikaner political thought: analysis and documents, Part 1* (with Andre du Toit, University of California Press). He is also editor and publisher of the political journal *Die Suid-Afrikaan.*

Prof Lawrence Schlemmer is director of the Centre for Policy Studies at the University of the Witwatersrand, a director and founding editor of the social science journal *Indicator South Africa*, published at the University of Natal, and vice-president and past president of the South African Institute of Race Relations. He has written widely in the field of political change, social attitudes and development studies, including *Change, reform and economic growth in SA* (with Eddie Webster, Ravan Press). He served on the constitutional committee of the KwaZulu-Natal Indaba.

THE AUTHORS (in order of appearance in table of contents)

Dr C J (Stoffel) van der Merwe at the time of writing was Deputy Minister of Information and of Constitutional Affairs. He is presently Cabinet Minister responsible for Information, Broadcasting Services and the Film Industry. He is a political scientist by training and has held academic posts at the Rand Afrikaans University.

Dr P J Steenkamp is a Member of Parliament. He is a mathematician by training and was previously a senior lecturer at the University of Natal. He served on the KwaZulu-Natal Indaba.

Jannie Gagiano lectures in the Department of Political Science at the University of Stellenbosch. He is well known for having conducted a range of political attitude studies among students since the seventies. He is currently examining the responses of South Africans to sanctions.

Mark Swilling is research officer at the Centre for Policy Studies, University of the Witwatersrand, and teaches in the Department of Political Studies at the same university. He is a well-known author in the field of black extra-parliamentary politics and a consultant to various extra-parliamentary movements and trade unions.

Paulus Zulu is a senior research fellow at the Centre of Social and Development Studies at the University of Natal and head of the Maurice Webb Race Relations Unit. In recent years he has specialised in the study of the dynamics of black political protest. He is also a member of the Institute for Black Research.

Dr F van Zyl Slabbert was leader of the Progressive Federal Party during the period when it was the Official Opposition in Parliament. He is a sociologist by training. Currently he is an honorary professor at the Graduate School of Business Administration, University of the Witwatersrand, and is the founder and policy director of the Institute for a Democratic Alternative for South Africa (IDASA).

Simon Jenkins is a former political editor of *The Economist* and is currently the editor of the *Sunday Times Literary Supplement* and a political columnist with the same paper. He serves on the Board of British Rail and is well known internationally as a commentator on international politics.

Prof Theodor Hanf is co-director of the Arnold Bergstraesser Institute in Freiburg, West Germany, and a professor at the University of Frankfurt. He is a specialist in the fields of politics and education and has written widely on deeply divided societies. He was the main author of *South Africa: the prospect for peaceful change*, which appeared in German and English some ten years ago (Kaiser-Grunewald Publishers and Rex Collings), an analysis which is currently being revised under his leadership.

NEGOTIATING SOUTH AFRICA'S FUTURE

DISCARDED

EDITORS

HERMANN GILIOMEE

LAWRENCE SCHLEMMER

In conjunction with

CENTRE FOR POLICY STUDIES
UNIVERSITY OF THE WITWATERSRAND

St. Martin's Press
NEW YORK

First published in the United States of America in 1989
Printed in Pretoria, Republic of South Africa

ISBN 0 312 03164 5

Library of Congress Cataloging-in-Publication Data

Negotiating South Africa's future

1. South Africa — Politics and government — 1978 -
2. South Africa — Constitutional history. I. Giliomee, Hermann Buhr, 1938 - . II. Schlemmer, Lawrence. III. University of the Witwatersrand. Centre for Policy Studies.

DT779.952.N44   1989   968.06   89-6430
ISBN 0 312 03164 5

CONTENTS

PREFACE

As will be indicated in the introductory chapter, this volume arose out of a sequence of events in the debate about an end to the political conflict in South Africa. The idea germinated in July 1987 in Dakar, Senegal, when the editors participated in discussions between members of the ANC and a group of academics and writers from South Africa. It received further impetus in the press debate which followed that event, and was given major substance at a symposium with the theme 'Political Accord in South Africa: Problems and Prospects', convened by the Centre for Policy Studies, Johannesburg, in January 1988. The contents of this volume reflect all these events since both a selection from the press debate in the *Sunday Times* and the proceedings of the symposium are covered here.

Having been participants in all these events and as academics with a long-standing interest in the issue of negotiation in South Africa, we as editors have attempted to explore the debate somewhat further in the concluding chapter. We do not presume to present any definitive conclusions, since this debate will continue for many years yet. Our intention is simply to raise possibilities for discussion.

Mobil South Africa assisted greatly in the project by contributing to the costs of the symposium. We would like to thank Mr Pat O'Malley, then with Mobil, for his enthusiastic support of the work. Hermann Giliomee wishes to thank the University of Cape Town for funding his research project on the nature of the conflict in South Africa.

We would like to express our appreciation to the participants in the symposium, some of whom travelled long distances to attend. We would also like to thank Dr Robin Lee, Colin Berkow, Sannette Roos, Carolyn Warren, Anitha van Heerden and other members of the staff of the Centre for Policy Studies, for their assistance in arranging, running and recording the proceedings of the Workshop. Colin Berkow's résumé of the discussions was most useful in preparing the penultimate chapter.

In particular we would like to thank the speakers at the symposium for their excellent papers, which form the bulk of this volume. Most of them are extremely busy people and the task of preparing their papers must have been a considerable burden on their time.

'Negotiation' is the subject of one of the more important research programmes of the Centre for Policy Studies. This volume is one of the first major products of this programme and we hope that it will be followed by other contributions to what might be the most important debate in South Africa.

HERMANN GILIOMEE
LAWRENCE SCHLEMMER

1

INTRODUCTION:
TOWARDS POLITICAL RESOLUTION IN
SOUTH AFRICA

The Editors

The debate about South Africa's political conflict and its future has always been a mixture of analysis, hope, despair and political posturing. On all sides of the conflict the importance of image, the need for political justification and a concern with the morale of one or other faction in the debate have caused terms to be abused, corrupted or usurped.

The term 'negotiation', the key to a future settlement, has itself fallen victim to the rhetoric of the interaction, and loose usage of bewildering proportions has been the result. Just as all parties claim to be 'democrats', so virtually all political contenders in the debate claim to be committed to negotiation. Even members of the Conservative Party, fundamentally committed to the total exclusion of blacks from political participation in white South Africa, at a recent conference in the USA stated their commitment to negotiating the terms of that exclusion.[1]

It would seem that the term 'negotiation', as used by various contenders to power in a future South Africa, is very widely interpreted. At one extreme we have the mere consultation of blacks by whites in regard to the conditions of their continued domination or of blacks' exclusion from power. At the other extreme are those who are interested only in white capitulation to the demands for unqualified majority rule. Perhaps the most misleading or futile use of the term comes from outside the ranks of the political actors – from well-meaning businessmen, churchmen and other part-time contributors to the debate who have the vague but fervent notion that 'talks', loosely defined, will magically unlock a process of reasonable compromise.

Upon analysis, this volume may well reflect some of these very same defects. At the same time, however, the focal point is on specific questions about South Africa's future which, we would hope, will lend somewhat greater definition to the conclusions drawn at the end. Our analysis is based on contributions made at a symposium held at the Centre for Policy Studies, Johannesburg, early in 1988.

The idea of the symposium was born after the editors had accompanied a group of largely white, Afrikaans-speaking 'internal' South Africans to

1

Dakar, Senegal, to have discussions with another group of South Africans, namely members of the exiled African National Congress. During and after this historic meeting certain ideas emerged which seemed to justify the initiation of a series of discussions on a negotiated resolution to the conflict in South Africa.

After the Dakar meeting, co-editor of this volume, Hermann Giliomee, in a newspaper article ('The Third Way', *Sunday Times*, 2 August 1987), concluded that a resolution could only be found in a high-level 'accord' between the principles of African and Afrikaner nationalism. The debate which ensued included critical rejoinders by Willem van Vuuren, Denis Worrall and Deputy Minister (now Minister) Stoffel van der Merwe. It concluded with a final assessment broadly supportive of Giliomee by Lawrence Schlemmer, co-editor of this volume. Brian Pottinger, deputy editor of the *Sunday Times*, also contributed to the debate, arguing that it could very well be too early for negotiation to succeed in South Africa. In a published reply to an open letter from Giliomee, Pallo Jordan of the ANC also responded to the basic notion of a 'Third Way' in the journal *Die Suid-Afrikaan*. The *Sunday Times* articles are included as chapter 2 in this volume. Because the government recently prohibited Jordan from being quoted in terms of security provisions, the exchange of letters between Giliomee and Jordan as they appeared in *Die Suid-Afrikaan*[2] cannot be republished here.

This volume used as a starting-point the symposium and the published debate referred to above, in an attempt at elaborating on the issues raised at the Dakar meeting. As such it is also an attempt at exploring, as exhaustively as possible, the impediments, opportunities and mechanisms relevant to a negotiated resolution of the South African conflict.

We suspect that our efforts may be interpreted as an attempt at finding a 'middle way', a compromise between the agendas of the government and the resistance movements, and that our intentions will be criticised by both sides. Our goal, however, is subtly but significantly different, best summed up by the title of Giliomee's article which sparked off the debate: 'The Third Way'.

Our intention is ambitious. It is most certainly not to qualify the fundamental commitments of those political movements which articulate the interests of the majority. Nor is it an attempt at formulating some or other compromise with apartheid. Our commitment as authors is fundamentally to a just participation in power by the majority in South Africa. We would have succeeded only should the proposals contained in the final chapters be able to accommodate the most basic political needs of all the people of South Africa.

The only reason we have chosen to deviate from the objective of immediate negotiations on the democratic enfranchisement of the majority is that we sense that this appeal in the current phase of South African political development is strategically unhelpful and unrealistic.

Politics in South Africa is frequently described as being in a situation of stalemate. While the government has stated a commitment to negotiation on power-sharing, there is very substantial divergence between its framework for the inclusion of all people in government and those of major movements opposing it from the left.

On the one hand, the government is committed to a position of power-sharing based on racially defined constituencies, thereby preserving for whites an unassailable power base and political self-determination in matters relating to the group. Central fiscal resources would have to be 'allocated' to groups, presumably involving mechanisms akin to those in a federation.

The external resistance movements, and those internal movements which support their broad goals, on the other hand, appear to be equally firmly committed to majority rule based on an undivided electorate. Any safeguards for minorities would be secondary to the principle of an open, non-racial electoral process. Such safeguards might involve a protection of certain interests but they certainly would not ensure group autonomy or group control over policy.

Between the two models a range of proposals has emerged in recent years, most of which embody some form of division or qualification of the process of majority choice, while at the same time rejecting any formal distinctions between race groups in the constitution. Such compromise models are usually described in forms of geographic federation, in the decentralisation of government to smaller regional or local units, or based on checks on the power of a majority-based legislature by second chambers.

Thus far, compromise proposals have not succeeded in winning acceptance from the government or the resistance movements. On the right they are perceived as not offering sufficiently strong guarantees of white minority participation and power parity in executive government. On the left they are viewed as strategies to perpetuate minority control and political privilege.

The KwaZulu-Natal Indaba proposals, for example, have been rejected both by government and by internal resistance movements on the grounds described.[3] While they may yet be implemented in one form or another, similar proposals for the country as a whole may be even more difficult for the government and perhaps even the resistance movements to accept.

This crystallisation of views is understandable. Black political actors and the resistance movements have become greatly alienated over decades of fruitless protest. They can hardly be expected not to mistrust the consequences of constitutional guarantees for white power. On the other hand, white interest groups, partly by virtue of decades of privileged control, have a great deal to lose, and tend to perceive themselves as potentially under dire threat of a decline in socio-economic standards, or of social and cultural victimisation.

3

The political distance between the two positions exemplifies the great difficulties impeding a resolution of conflict. There are a range of conditions for negotiation which are highly problematic in South Africa, to say the least. Serious negotiation between contending parties in a political conflict would seem to need the following conditions:

- A rough symmetry in the balance of power between the major participants. As the established government of the country, the major white political formation clearly controls formal power resources far beyond that which the ANC or other extra-parliamentary movements are likely to possess for the foreseeable future. Internal and external challenges to the legitimacy and capacity of the State to govern have not succeeded in significantly weakening the ability of the State to maintain its coherence, its ability to collect taxes, to maintain broad administrative control in crucial areas of society, or to ensure compliance by force if necessary. The resistance movements have considerable symbolic resources derived from their large popular following, but these represent resources very different to those of government. Theirs are the resources which will ensure permanent unease and a sense of crisis in South Africa. As Tamarkin[4] suggests, the two sets of resources are not necessarily unequal in effect, but it is difficult for the participants to recognise this because they have totally different power bases.

- A mutual willingness to accept goals which can be reconciled. The South African government has repeatedly confirmed that its bottom line in negotiation is the protection of self-determination for whites over major areas of white community life and that self-determination is to be secured in perpetuity by a separate political mobilisation of whites. Most of the black or extra-parliamentary or external movements fundamentally reject the proviso to the general democratic process that white self-determination would imply.

- Cohesive organisation among the negotiating formations so that little danger exists of the support organisation fragmenting under the strain of compromises which all negotiation implies. The white negotiating groups, as parliamentary organisations, have the cohesion required, as do, perhaps, Inkatha and the trade unions. Many of the resistance movements are mobilised for protest rather than for participation in processes of give and take. Their unity may not reflect a genuine coherence of interests beyond that of opposing the system. Of particular importance would be the ability of the resistance movements to control radicals within their own ranks during negotiation. No clear indication is available at this stage.

- Access to defined constituencies so that compromises and positions during negotiation can be tested. Once again the white formations and Inkatha have this facility. The resistance movements, on the other hand, partly because of the destruction of their organisations by State action and partly because of the absence of formal mobilising activity, do not have organisational access to their constituencies. The independent trade unions are an exception, but, a certain measure of political rhetoric notwithstanding, these organisations are not mobilised around political objectives, and there are indications from substantial surveys of black worker opinion that the many members would break ranks on political issues. The union federations do appear to have a strong political theme on their agendas but they are not directly answerable to grass roots constituencies.

- Trust in the negotiation framework. An established government which does not perceive that its sheer survival is threatened, is not likely to join in building a negotiation process which it does not control. On the other hand, it cannot be expected of resistance movements to readily enter into negotiations organised by the major opponent. For this reason commentators often suggest an 'honest broker' role for external powers, as happened in the Lancaster House talks on Rhodesia. For major parts of the white constituency, however, no external power is likely to be seen as sufficiently objective to play this role.

- Also, perhaps, both sides, in terms of their internal cohesion, would see more gains than losses by entering into negotiation. Both the ANC/UDF and NP would possibly fear break-aways if they entered into negotiations which carried the implication of compromise.

- Above all, perhaps, both sides should perceive no realistic alternative to even-handed negotiation and substantial compromise. The white government in South Africa, however, could maintain viability as an established administration for some time yet, if for no other reason than its overriding police and military superiority and sufficient economic autonomy to survive external pressures. Among the resistance movements, the rather naked exclusion from power of the majority, the precedents of liberation elsewhere in Africa, the weight of international moral support and a marked demographic advantage inside South Africa, might constantly suggest that the perceived iniquity of the system cannot possibly survive. These perceptions, if true, virtually cancel out the possibility of compromise-based negotiations.

These and other requirements and conditions are so far removed from the reality of the South African situation that a debate on a negotiated resolution might seem futile in advance. There are, however, indications in the society that might be grounds for greater optimism.

Ours is not a society in which the contending groups are locked into little more than a struggle for survival or the protection of sectional interests. Since World War II South Africa has experienced general growth in prosperity and quality of life. Although there has been a decline in standards of living over the past decade, particularly for middle- and lower-middle-class whites in relative terms, both whites and blacks realise and can anticipate the fact that alternatives to a grim struggle for political supremacy are achievable. In other words, the positive benefits of a negotiated settlement have a popular appeal which must to some degree influence the stances which political leaders may take. Day to day interaction between members of different political communities are also much more cordial and relaxed than in, say, Lebanon, Northern Ireland, Cyprus, Sri Lanka or other deeply divided conflict societies. In other words, in South Africa's case the prospects exist for a mobilisation of popular enthusiasm for a settlement which could outweigh the negative conditions discussed above.

Furthermore, in this country with its large and sophisticated industrial base, there are private sector interests which would benefit enormously from a settlement of the political conflict and which could, if appropriately organised, facilitate a negotiation process. These general factors would make a careful analysis of the prospects for a negotiated resolution infinitely worthwhile.

In our view, the following external conditions could facilitate the negotiation process.

- A 'principle of compromise', if effectively promoted, might open up a willingness to negotiate on an open-ended basis where it would not otherwise exist. The idea of a 'third way', discussed very broadly in the articles published in the *Sunday Times*, and which preceded this analysis, is perhaps one example of such a mobilising principle.
- South Africa has very polarised political goals in the ultimate sense, but it is not necessarily a deeply polarised society in all respects. Numerous empirical studies[5] reveal the extent to which convergent attitudes to the political future exist between the different racial and ethnic communities. This common ground could form the basis for effective political alliances, which in a 'bottom-up' process could begin to narrow the gap between the more starkly polarised positions taken by the major political movements.
- Interim or transitional initiatives, such as negotiations on local issues or even regional settlements, could very well illustrate the extent to which compromises are possible once a process commences.
- While there are elements in the political interaction and in the security administration in South Africa which at present may constantly create impediments to negotiation, there may be ways in which these effects could be avoided if all sides were to become more conscious of the need to establish a climate for negotiations. Not only administration and security action is at issue. The quality and flavour of political rhetoric is important, and relevant on both sides of the conflict.

These are the kinds of issues and problems which will be debated in subsequent chapters. These issues contain two major components, both essential to political resolution, namely, issues of goals, or put differently, constitutional content; and issues of process – the way in which decision-making and political interaction at present can facilitate or retard negotiation at a later stage. Goals and process are not presented in a specific order in the text, but we will attempt to separate these elements in the concluding chapter.

Finally, a brief comment about the issues of compromise. Apartheid has acquired extremely negative connotations both within South Africa and in the world at large. This makes it very problematic to talk of a compromise between the ethnic and material interests of whites, and the interests of the majority of South Africans. We are not insensitive to this. On the other hand we feel strongly that the costs of failing to find a compromise are so high that sensitivities cannot dictate our political discourse. Without a compromise South Africans of all colours and classes face endless struggle. The white-controlled system has in recent years not only survived the worst internal protest and violent resistance in South African history but has emerged with a much more sophisticated security policy than before. External pressures can lower the rate of economic growth very considerably but they also tend to increase the reliance of the economy on government. They also weaken creative political variety among white interest groups. The present phase of relative calm illustrates the fact that active resistance in South Africa proceeds in cycles; there is not necessarily an ineluctable progression towards the overthrow of the existing power-structure.

A debate on compromise may seem insensitive to the genuine and understandable moral commitments of the resistance movements, but any such insensitivity is unintentional. A conciliation of the present commitments of the major contending parties is based on humanitarian considerations – the avoidance of several more decades of political frustration, loss of shared prosperity and – worse still – cycles of violence and bloodshed.

NOTES
[1] Comments made by prominent Conservative Party spokesmen (MPs) at a private conference on a future political and socio-economic dispensation for South Africa at the Institute for Contemporary Studies (San Francisco), Williamsburg, USA, 7 – 10 April 1988.
[2] 'Briefwisseling oor Dakar', *Die Suid-Afrikaan*, vol 13, Feb. 1988, p 22 *passim*.
[3] See the range of articles in *Indicator South Africa, New Frontiers: The KwaZulu-Natal Debates*, Durban: University of Natal, October 1987.
[4] Mordechai Tamarkin, 'A Path to Peace', *Leadership SA*, vol 5, no 4, p 18 *et seq*.
[5] See, for example, C P de Kock, 'Possible implications of the election on the escalation and de-escalation of violence in South Africa', in D J van Vuuren, L Schlemmer, J Latakgomo, and H C Marais, *South African election 1987*, Pinetown: Owen Burgess, pp 319 – 328.

PART I

2

THE PRESS DEBATE

Selections from the debate in the Sunday Times *during August and September 1987, which stimulated the symposium and the contributions which form the basis of this volume.*

THE THIRD WAY

Hermann Giliomee

One of the rare gains of the political turmoil which has gripped South Africa since September 1984 is the growing perception that the country can no longer postpone a decision about its political course. In Clem Sunter's terms, we have an inescapable choice between a Low Road of authoritarian co-optation and endemic violence, and a High Road of genuine negotiations, stability and economic growth. As this perception has grown, the Nationalist Government and the ANC leadership, as the two main adversaries, have embarked on an urgent search for a formula which will put it at the helm of the journey along their version of the High Road.

In the case of the National Party, there is the desperate desire for a clever technical formula which would grant continued control, but which would also persuade the masses that their material needs are being addressed by an increasingly multi-racial government.

As the ANC shifts its emphasis from the military to the political terrain, it seeks a powerful universal principle which will be so attractive that large numbers in the opposition camp will either cross to its side or resign themselves to defeat.

In their hearts, whites know that peace and prosperity in the 1990s and beyond will not be born out of a clever technical formula. We realise that the only road to peace lies through genuine negotiations. What is seldom realised, however, is that before the main contending forces can embark on meaningful negotiations, they must clear the first and most difficult hurdle: *they must agree on the very nature of the conflict.*

The resolution of conflicts between managements and workers is possible exactly because both parties agree that the conflict is an economic one over the marginal distribution of profits. By contrast, political conflicts are much more difficult to define. Yet such a definition is indispensable. Unless the contending parties can agree on this question, unending strife is a foregone conclusion. Press attention to the Dakar *Indaba* between an ANC delegation and a group of internal South Africans has focused on the discussions over violence.

More significant, however, was the rivalry between different interpretations of the nature of the South African conflict. The absence of a consensus over this issue forms a major stumbling-block to joint strategies in the common struggle against apartheid or to real negotiations getting under way.

In Dakar I contended, against strong opposition, that the conflict in South Africa was not primarily an apartheid-induced one between a privileged white and a disadvantaged black group. Nor is it a class struggle between a white bourgeoisie and a black working class. It is rather a communal conflict in which Afrikaner and African nationalists, with the National Party and the ANC in the respective vanguards, struggle for control over the same historic homeland.

To some extent, communal conflicts such as those in South Africa, Israel, Lebanon, Cyprus, Northern Ireland and Sri Lanka resemble international conflicts. The opposing sides contest not only a disputed territory, they also believe that national sovereignty, integrity and honour are at stake. The sides have their own armies and stormtroops, symbols and songs, heroes and martyrs, *verraaiers* and *impimpis*.

But, in a vital way, communal conflicts differ from international conflicts, making them much more intractable. In international conflicts and negotiations, the adversaries respect each other as legitimate, autonomous entities. In communal conflicts, however, the competing national entities refuse to accord the other the dignity of a respectable foe, much less accept them as a negotiating partner. The reason is simple: once they accept the nationalist credentials of the other side, they relativise, and thus jeopardise, their claim to sovereign authority over their homeland. Accordingly, the discourse between the NP and ANC leadership has been restricted to attempts to demonise each other.

President Botha has sought to portray the ANC as a despicable band of terrorists led and inspired by communists, waging war on the peace-loving people of South Africa. And Mr Oliver Tambo projects the Pretoria regime as a fascist gang of reactionary racists who suppress the hopes and aspirations of all the progressive people of South Africa.

On the one hand, the government's attempts at co-opting black leaders in a white-controlled system have been a major affront to all black nationalists, who deeply resent the underlying assumption that they could be bought off through patronage and slightly improved material conditions. On the other hand, we have the ANC which believes that whites are merely clinging to their privileges and other rewards of the apartheid system. It is exactly because the ANC ignores the strength of Afrikaner nationalism and a larger white group consciousness that it can believe that victory is inevitable. It confidently expects that upper-class whites can be persuaded to think their property and other survival interests will be better protected by an ANC government strongly committed to the principle of non-racialism. The ANC anticipates that, as it steps up the pressure, the upper-class whites will turn against the regime which will have no alternative but to opt for a negotiated settlement and allow majority rule.

Finally, it is believed that the main problem of an ANC government will be to find an alternative livelihood for white civil servants who will be replaced in the inevitable Africanisation of the civil service – other whites will rejoice that the struggle is over. In this scheme of thinking, the ANC reduces Afrikaner ethnicity to a quaint and archaic relic. A Dakar and ANC delegate, Pallo Jordan, observed in a recent newspaper article that the Afrikaner nationalist intelligentsia have adopted an 'anti-modernist' ideology or posture, which celebrates the 'dubious virtues of *volk, kerk* and family'. Sadly, this perspective ignores virtually the entire serious literature of the last 25 years, not only on the politics of South Africa but on communal conflicts throughout the world, which strongly rejects the interpretation that nationalism is an obsolete ideology and political strategy in modern industrial societies.

In the early 1960s social scientists still believed that there would be a shift away from ethnic-based to class-based politics. Unfortunately, the very opposite has happened. As Harvard's Nathan Glazer remarked: ethnicity now looks like a universal force with a power to move people, that is putting class – 'rational' interest, if one uses an oversimple distinction, as against the 'irrational' traditional forces of peoplehood, language and religion – in the shade.

Ethno-nationalism, of which the Afrikaners are a salient example, is in fact a very modern phenomenon, employed universally by groups to assert themselves in the urban environment. It enjoys a great advantage as a form of political mobilisation for the simple reason that – whether it be in the extreme form of the Conservative Party or the milder form of the NP – it manages to combine a deep emotional attachment to the ethnic (or broader white) group and its perceived homeland with the promotion of defence of the discrete class interests of the members of the group.

Some of the ANC delegates at Dakar seemed to scoff at this. They believed whites would increasingly be more worried about their immediate physical and material well-being than their nationalist concerns.

Yet all the evidence from communal conflicts elsewhere points the other way. As the strife continues, the ethnic commitments tend to intensify, not weaken. Invariably the parties understand the conflict in terms of 'survival' which goes much beyond physical survival or material well-being to the basic issues of a group's political status and identity, and to their existential fears of annihilation or 'bloodbaths'.

Not much store should be put upon rationality when ethnic groups are pushed to the wall. Theo Hanf, a German expert on communal conflicts, warned: 'It is by no means certain that economic considerations would govern the behaviour of a dominant group if it felt – rightly or wrongly is immaterial to the consequences – that its existence was threatened ... A scorched-earth policy is not an economically rational concept. Nevertheless it is one often, and particularly practised in civil wars between ethnic or religious groups.'

When President Botha says that the Afrikaners have resolved never to be subordinate again, no one should ignore the deadly intent behind those words of the man and his likely successors.

If the ANC is serious about emphasising political strategies rather than the armed struggle, it should seriously reconsider its opposition to white group representation and to a power-sharing compromise.

One can depict the politics of South Africa as comprising two power blocs: one based on the ethno-nationalism of the Africans, and the other on the larger white community. The essence of ethno-nationalism to South Africa and elsewhere is the self-identification of a people with a group – its past, its present and, most importantly, its destiny. Short of military defeat – which is unlikely, to say the least – the great majority of whites in general and the Afrikaners in particular will insist on choosing their own leaders. Only such leaders, heading a 'group-centred' political community (which may well include strata of coloureds, Indians and blacks), will be able to legitimise to their white constituency the sweeping changes which South Africa will have to undergo in the next two decades. They may include integration of residential areas, the desegregation of schools, the 'blackening' of central government and recasting of national goals and symbols.

Another large political bloc which has crystallised in recent years in South Africa is comprised of the majority of people who rightly resent being compelled to participate in politics along prescribed 'ethnic' lines. A flexible political strategy could soon put the ANC at the head of this political bloc – one based on African nationalism but also genuinely committed to non-racialism. It would challenge ethnicity used as a cloak for privilege but would accept that there could be legitimate forms of group rights and group representation.

A proposal for a form of bicommunalism built on these two blocs does not spring from conservative or nationalist convictions, but rather from the wish to prevent South Africa from walking the entire grisly course of other communal conflicts.

However, before any political accommodation can be found, the NP and ANC will first have to accept the struggle as a communal one in which the adversaries have the power to inflict untold damage upon each other, and on the economy, without any clear victor emerging.

(*Sunday Times*, 2 August 1987)

NOT JUST TWO GROUPS

Stoffel van der Merwe

The best decisions in life – and in politics – are those that are based upon the facts as they are and not on the 'facts' as someone wishes them to be. For this reason I welcome the basic insights contained in Hermann Giliomee's article – although I do not agree with his conclusions. Giliomee's basic thesis is that the conflict in South Africa is in essence what he calls a 'communal conflict' and not primarily a racial conflict as it is often described, nor a class conflict as the ANC or the SACP would want it to be in order to fit their ancient social theories. The 'communal conflict' is not much different from what one would normally describe as a conflict between groups, each with its own nationalistic aspirations.

A further useful insight is that 'to some extent communal conflicts ... resemble international conflicts'. Europe is a piece of real estate roughly comparable in size to that of South Africa, that has been inhabited for centuries by a number of cultural groups about as numerous and diverse as those of modern South Africa. In the absence of the queasiness and the preoccupation with human rights that are the hallmarks of the 20th century, the tribes of Europe fought many wars, effected many forced removals and extinguished many lives in a centuries-long process in which each group was eventually consolidated into a nation and owned its own piece of land in which it became a sovereign nation-state.

By the second half of the 20th century the stage was reached where each of these groups was reasonably safe behind international boundaries and its right to self-determination more or less guaranteed. Under the cover of this luxurious overall safety of the group, these nations could devote all their attention to safeguarding the rights of individuals against the overpowering might of the State.

It is interesting to note, however, that in times of war – when the overall safety of the group is threatened – it is regarded as legitimate to move individual rights to the deep background until such time as the danger to the group as such has been averted.

In the normal European situation, one can thus discern two levels of politics: one at which the safety of the group is guaranteed (international politics) and one at which the individual is protected against the might of the State (domestic politics). No wonder, therefore, that Hermann Giliomee discerns a likeness to international politics in what he calls 'communal conflict'.

For some reason the people in South Africa (perhaps because of less aggressive natures?) fought far fewer wars and exterminated far fewer people than their counterparts in Europe, North America or Australia. (The longest and most destructive war in our history was fought against a European power, anyway.) For a long time they furthermore practised a far less rigid form of separation than on those continents, with the result that the various groups came to form a much more integrated pattern of settlement than for instance in Europe.

Whereas in Europe each nation protected its own territory jealously and forcefully against settlement by other groups, the people in South Africa mingled almost carelessly, with the result that members of most groups are scattered throughout the subcontinent in large numbers. As a consequence of this, the problem has arisen that the potential for conflict between groups cannot be handled at the level of international politics and with the aid of international boundaries. Indeed, the challenge of South Africa is to handle both levels of politics (that between groups and between the State and the individual) within the bounds of one political system, i.e. at the level of domestic politics.

If Hermann Giliomee is correct when he says that 'to some extent, communal conflicts … resemble international conflicts', then it surely follows logically that the solution to the problem must also, to some extent, resemble international political solutions. This, I believe, is a very valuable insight into the South African situation. I have, however, some difficulties with certain facets of Giliomee's further analysis. One is that it amounts to an oversimplification of the situation.

If indeed it was only a communal conflict between two opposing nationalisms, the solution could perhaps have been as relatively simple as that of the late Dr Verwoerd. The fact is that the situation is complicated by a meeting of the First and the Third World, by racial connotations which are problematical everywhere in the world, by the fact that even within particular groups huge differences have developed between traditional and modernized sections, and by the many cultural problems that stem from the disruptive effects of urbanisation on the original cultural patterns.

The second problem with Giliomee's analysis is that he sees it simply as a conflict between two nationalisms – i.e. between 'Afrikaner and African nationalists'. This leads him to the conclusion that the solution lies in a 'form of bicommunalism', whatever that may be when it is translated into a political system. But it is a fallacy to disregard the many cultural divisions in the ranks of what he glibly terms as 'Africans'. (After more than ten generations I regard myself as 'African' as any other African.) The mistake of disregarding the group loyalties of, for instance, the Zulus, the Xhosas or the Tswanas, will be at the cost of a peaceful future.

A third problem which flows from the previous oversimplifications is that he simply sees the National Party and the ANC as 'in the respective vanguards' of the two nationalisms which he identifies. From this he deduces that the solution lies in these two organisations coming to some arrangement. Oversimplification again. The fact is that the ANC with its quaintly un-African socialist philosophies cannot hope to accommodate the various aspirations of all the groups in South Africa. One scientific study

15

after the other shows that yes, a large number (but not a majority) of black people hold the ANC in high symbolic esteem; but no, up to 80 per cent of black people see no future in their declared policies of violent revolution or State socialism. The ANC certainly has its supporters, but so have many other black leaders and organisations.

The real lesson of the French, the Russian and many other revolutions is that violent revolution does not bring democracy, but instead retards it by decades, if not by a century or more. It makes no sense to try to cohabit with people who deal in violence if the aim which one pursues is democracy – a system which is essentially based upon the assumption of the peaceful settlement of political disputes.

I thank Giliomee, however, for his insight that the sole motivation of Afrikaners (and whites in general) is not to prevent the loss of their material 'privileges'. In fact it goes much, much deeper.

The one thing that equals the Afrikaners' determination to safeguard the future of their own cultural heritage is their determination to create a future dispensation that will be experienced as a just system by all who live in it. If we simply exchanged one form of domination for another form of domination we would have gained very little, if anything. If we can develop a society in which a variety of groups can live together without any group or any significant number of individuals experiencing it as an oppressive system, then that would be progress. That is the ideal to which we are committed.

(*Sunday Times*, 9 August 1987)

A NEW ICE AGE?

Brian Pottinger

The most unfair criticism of President Botha's political style must surely be that it is inconsistent. Since May last year – the month when the Eminent Persons initiative collapsed and South Africa's Prague Spring officially came to an end – the President has been unerringly constant. Adaptive reform, he has insisted, must be accompanied by a stable domestic situation: it is impossible to have the former without the latter. But it is in the practical application of this otherwise unexceptional proposition that much of the dilemma now lies.

Like the slow passage of an ice-breaker, Mr Botha batters his way through the political floes rarely, it would appear, considering if they can be skirted or even partly melted. Thoughts of ice floes occur naturally enough in the wake of the President's vote this week which, although not as symbolically important as Rubicon or as materially significant as his September 30, 1985 speech (one country, one constitution, one citizenship) is noteworthy enough to warrant some close study.

The two themes of the National Party's post-referendum period emerged again clearly this week. First, the government intends drawing up the constitutional menu, and even if most of the guests decline, the government will be content to seat the remnants, no matter whom. Bon appétit.

Second, those not gracious enough to join the table can expect no mercy from the State: not their persons, their organisations, their media or even their sympathisers. In a classic formulation of the most dog-eared trick in the Handbook of Authoritarian Government, Mr Botha declared this week that those who are not with the National Party are against it – and by extension with the revolution.

The constitutional question first: two crucial tests await the government's attempt to draw blacks into its compartmentalised political process, or what the Pretoria apparatchiks call, with no apparent sense of irony, 'broadening the base of democracy'.

The first is the local government elections scheduled for October 1988, and the second is election of black representatives to the National Statutory Council – a sort of revamped version of the Native Representatives Council which Dr Hendrik Verwoerd so enthusiastically scrapped in 1956.

The prognosis for black participation appears fairly bad, and in that there should be little grounds for satisfaction by anybody. As much as Mr Botha's uncompromising political style is at fault in failing to provide the opening for credible black leadership to come forward, so also to blame is the radical left's congenital lack of tactical sense which prevents them from seizing the platforms to oppose the government. What remains is not, however, an encouraging scenario.

In the short term the government will negotiate only with those blacks who make themselves available. There are already ominous indications that some state agencies are going out of their way to help create 'legitimacy' for various peripatetic and often dubious township figures simply so that the government will have the pretence of somebody to engage – real 'mirror, mirror on the wall' stuff, but without the surprise ending. Black radical politicians, meanwhile, will no doubt call for boycotts of the elections and turn in pretty good results.

That one-off point made, they will again retreat into a muttering political impotency while the elected figures pretend to make the running, but, if precedent is anything to go by, will devote themselves to narrower, shall we say more personal, interests.

Is there a way around this ice floe?

That raises the second point which has engaged much heated debate in recent months and is now a topic pretty well flogged to death, but not quite – not least of all because of the government's insistence in keeping it alive.

With whom should the government negotiate? The suggestion that Mr Botha negotiates directly with the African National Congress is no longer practicable; it is perhaps not even desirable at this point. There are a number of reasons for this: the refusal, or inability, of the ANC to suspend the armed struggle; the National Party's cynical damaging but successful demonisation of the ANC to obscure its own political deficiencies; the obsessive security force view of communist influence in acts of even mild and legal resistance. Historically we have reached a point where even the prospect of recognising the ANC is anathema to the majority of whites, although this need not have been.

Having created those conditions, the government, by the force of its own logic, must now abide by the consequences: one of these being that even if it wanted to open channels to the ANC, its constituency will now not let it. That is a reality and radicals would do well to at least confront it.

In a recent article in the American magazine *Commentary*, sociologists Peter Berger and Anglo's Bobby Godsell raise the intriguing question of whether South Africa's dilemma is not that it is too late for negotiations, but perhaps too early. There is much truth in that: neither Pretoria nor a diasporic ANC have inflicted sufficient damage on each other although, in truth, the military component of the ANC/comrades struggle has been severely dented by the scale and ferocity of the State counter-assault.

It is in this uneasy interval that the groundwork could be laid for an eventual accommodation (solution is too presumptious a word). However, it is a long step from this to suggesting immediate and unconditional negotiations between Mr Botha and Oliver Tambo. It is thus rather in the prospects for atmosphere creation (forgive the sociology-speak) that our greatest hope must lie.

But we immediately encounter a problem of perspective. The right wing and the government would argue that moves aimed at engaging the extra-parliamentary left creates the atmosphere for white capitulation, nothing less, while a reformist view holds that it creates an atmosphere of compromise.

The first view suggests a serious lack of faith in the strength of one's own arguments and the wiles of one's negotiators, while the second implies almost super-human qualities of skill, patience and faith. Yet it is in the latter option that a happier future surely lies. The lesson most often taught in the last dramatic years, and as regularly ignored by the government, is that the wider and more indiscriminate the repression, the more powerful the unifying factor among the resistance.

The United Democratic Front, the Congress of South African Trade Unions and even, to an extent, the African National Congress, are affiliations of loosely defined viewpoints and philosophies. The UDF, certainly, is an unlikely grouping of tactics and philosophies united mostly by the need to survive against the all-embracing State attack – more than one UDF and Cosatu leader has made this point.

Where once a flexible and sensitive government might have driven a fleet of ideological Casspirs between the main players, they opted in the first instance for the real ones. Which brings us back to Mr Botha and his vote.

The view that mere recognition of the role of the ANC and the extra-parliamentary radical left under present conditions is traitorous, is not only silly, it is dangerous. Isolating and demonising the UDF made the organisation not politically weaker, but stronger. If the government cannot politically afford to be seen engaging the ANC or the extra-parliamentary left, it could at least temper its rhetoric and obsession for control so as to allow others to try and establish the bridgeheads. They might just be needed in the future.

(Sunday Times, 16 August 1987)

MANY 'ISRAELS', NO SOLUTIONS

Denis Worrall

Hermann Giliomee's view that the underlying conflict in South Africa is not a racial one or a class or (presumably) even a simple moral one but a communal one between black African and Afrikaner nationalism is, of course, not original. Twenty years ago Professor Ned Munger wrote a book contrasting Afrikaner and African nationalism, and this has been a theme in much writing about South Africa.

In fact, Adam and Moodley, in their excellent analysis, *South Africa without apartheid* (1986), regard the mutual respect between Afrikaner and black African nationalism as one of the hopeful aspects of the situation: the issue is not the conquest or withdrawal of one of the parties (as is the case in colonial situations) but the terms and conditions of their co-existence.

Giliomee's article is therefore less important for its originality than for its timing.

The failure of the P W Botha government to project any vision or sense of direction, the resulting growth of right-wing sentiment, the increase in violence and growing doubts among both blacks and whites about the likelihood of peaceful answers justify a frank discussion of this issue and the nature of conflict generally.

The modern political history of South Africa is the story of the rise to power of Afrikaner nationalism. The Afrikaner has slowly but surely imposed his values and way of looking at the world on South African society. He has moulded the symbols of State according to his history and deeply influenced the institutions of government.

In race relations, apartheid, as conceived by the likes of Paul Sauer and SABRA (South African Bureau for Racial Affairs) academics, was intended as a fair strategy to ensure general racial harmony and Afrikaner survival. It was the Afrikaner nationalist response to decolonisation and independence.

On the analogy of Israel, which (it is said) gave a sense of security to Jews in the Diaspora, everybody in South Africa was to have his Israel. And, indeed, between history and government policy, every black 'nation' has got an Israel of kinds, but the whites (and the Afrikaners in particular), the coloureds and the Indians now find themselves completely outnumbered, competing in the black Diaspora and without territories of their own.

The strategy failed at tremendous cost in terms of human suffering, civil liberties, time and money. The black tide to the cities was not turned around. Professor Sakkie Fourie's prophecy about 'economic integration' became a reality.

The most poignant expression of the failure of the strategy is what the 'Oranje-werkers' are striving for – an Afrikaans Israel. But much more important than the reaction of the Oranje-werkers is how Afrikaner leaders presently in government will respond when the political realities of our situation make themselves felt.

The Afrikaners' achievements are considerable and it is possibly understandable that the identification between Afrikaner (and white) interest and the State is taken for granted. But what happens when this is challenged? Do Afrikaner politicians have the philosophical basis to identify with a broad South Africanism? Or will they turn to their roots and mobilise Afrikaner sentiment? And if this is what they do, on what terms will they mobilise Afrikaners? Will it be on a basis of language and culture and history – the traditional source of nationalism and something which is universally understood and accepted? Or will it be on a basis of colour and race – something which in the last quarter of the 20th century is universally rejected?

What the rest of us think may be relevant, but this is central and will be decisive in determining how our political future is shaped. Identifying the underlying nature of our conflict is one thing; gaining political acceptance is another thing altogether.

It is part of Hermann Giliomee's argument that, having recognised the nature of the conflict, it must be accommodated in the political solution. This is a view which is rejected by many black leaders and most black organisations. And it is an argument that is not going to be settled by articles in newspapers.

Most political leaders in South Africa, including the leaders of the National Party, have come to accept that a new system of government for South Africa cannot be left to one party or even one section of the population. It will be the result of the interaction of the numerous major points of view represented in our society.

I believe a first step in getting this process going is to spell out in an independent and neutral way all the major constitutional choices before us. In this way the level of the debate will be raised and in this way people will get a sense of security which they do not presently have. White South Africans, for example, will see that fundamental political change does not mean going from the present system to one person, one vote in a unitary State.

However, the lesson of all the National Party's failed attempts at getting negotiations going is that the neutral starting-point for this process must be created outside existing institutions of government. This is a process into which the natural aspirations of all communities – and especially those presently defined by law – would be released.

Is there a so-called 'coloured' identity or not? And, if so, what are its values? How correct is it to say that there are individual black identities? And how strong are they?

An Afrikaner nationalism defined in terms of language and culture (much as N P van Wyk Louw defined it in *Liberale Nasionalisme)* would have a moral foundation and would be in a position to demand that its right to self-determination should be recognised. It certainly would have the right to be recognised in any serious negotiation process regarding the political future of this country. Indeed, such a process is arguably vital to the expression of such an Afrikaner nationalism – given the fact that it is being drowned out by an ideological mix of white racism and white nationalism – neither of which has a sustaining moral base and both of which are recipes for disaster.

Aside from the conflict of nationalism aspect, there are other almost as pressing reasons for adopting this approach to our diversity. The government knows that its concept of 'own' affairs, group areas and racially segregated schools are all being challenged increasingly.

If we are to end apartheid, the Population Registration Act and group membership by law have to go and be replaced by voluntary association. This applies within white South Africa and works very well.

The prospect of releasing natural community aspirations in this kind of process is an exciting one because it is premised on a vision of a South Africa which works for all its people, a vision of a South Africa which is democratic and in which human dignity for all South Africans is recognised; and a vision of a South Africa which is fully accepted by the international community.

(Sunday Times, 23 August 1987)

DIFFERENT CULTURES, YES, RACIAL DOMINATION, NO

Willem van Vuuren

Defining the nature of the conflict in South Africa as essentially a struggle between opposing nationalisms raises some troublesome questions.

Firstly, it tends to ideologise the problem by obscuring the more brutal Machiavellian aspects of National Party rule as a source of conflict. It lends itself to interpretations that present the repressive self-preservation of a minority regime as something quite natural and innocent, even admirable, as a noble, culturally inspired struggle against threatening rival nationalisms. As such, Nationalist domination can be presented as an expression of

21

'the Afrikaners' determination to safeguard the future of their own cultural heritage', to quote Deputy Minister Stoffel van der Merwe.

However, against this idealistic interpretation, it can more historically be argued that the Botha government does not seek or employ power as a means to serve its less innocent power interests. While the NP clearly appreciates the strategic value of Afrikaner nationalism as a mobilising force, the government's decision-making hardly seems to be motivated by Afrikaner nationalist sentiments. Its past and recent record speaks rather of a propensity to view Afrikaner culture in terms of selfish party political interests, i.e. to subordinate what is culturally valuable to Afrikaners to what is politically useful to Nationalists.

Nationalists, who have always noisily expressed their patriotic concern about the future of the Afrikaans language, have also been quite prepared to accept the cultural alienation of millions of Afrikaans-born 'nie-blankes' for political reasons.

Secondly, the nationalisms thesis not only elevates the conflict to a normal and acceptable cultural struggle, but gives rise to concern about the future of Afrikaner culture that obfuscates the more immediate present conditions threatening that future. It induces a self-centred, inward-looking attitude among Afrikaners which is expressed by an insistence on guarantees for their group rights, safeguards for their cultural heritage and their right to self-determination.

The implicit assumption underlying such collective egocentrism is that the future possibility of a black majority government constitutes the biggest threat to Afrikaner culture. Should they not rather be concerned about the threat posed by the present white minority government? That is, about a regime whose desperate attempts at self-preservation are systematically undermining the few remaining conditions for a better future for all of us.

If Afrikaners are determined 'to create a future dispensation that will be experienced as a just system by all who live in it', as Dr van der Merwe believes, it must now be practically demonstrated. It is the actual holders of power that must be pressurised into working constructively towards a culturally tolerant and democratic dispensation, not the possible future power holders.

Thirdly, besides fostering the dangerous illusion that the threat to cultural self-determination and democratic group rights lies beyond Nationalist domination, the theoretical description of the conflict as a clash of nationalisms leads to prescriptive formulas which have already failed in practice. Surely, we do not need the further constitutional entrenchment of group divisions, in the form of Bantustans, tricameral parliament, or whatever. One can accept the reality of group divisions without officially promoting it. The conflict in South Africa is not generated by the existence of different cultures or interest groups as such, but rather by the oppression and frustration they suffer under a profoundly undemocratic political system.

Instead of dreaming about the 'just' accommodation of conflicting nationalisms, we should rather begin to practise the genuine deracialisation and democratisation of our politics.

It is helpful of Dr van der Merwe to point out that 'if we simply exchange one form of domination for another form of domination we will have gained very little, if anything'. At least that confirms the existing situation as one of domination. However, the problem is that his party's policy to gradually cast the net of co-optation a bit wider, does not offer a democratic alternative to the oppressive status quo. On the contrary, instead of broadening democracy it serves to broaden the ethnic base of Nationalist domination.

Instead of any real movement towards democratic government, the general drift is towards totalitarian control with increasing emphasis of the negative and destructive aspects of crisis-management: the entrenchment of emergency rule, more threats, more bannings and more restrictions on non-violent opposition. If we consider the government's paranoid attitude towards the 'outside world', 'hostile' international media, 'revolution-exporting' neighbours, and examine its Total Onslaught propaganda in defence of domestic oppression, then analogies drawn from ethnic conflicts in Northern Ireland, Cyprus, etc., seem less relevant than a critical understanding of the Machiavellian power conflicts that led to disaster in Stalinist Russia and the Third Reich. During the most destructive stages of these histories, the conflict manifested itself in systemic domination rather than some form of cultural self-assertion.

The structural-institutional changes that accompanied the growth of unchecked government powers soon reduced lofty ideals and nationalist aspirations to mere appendages of selfish strategic interests. Power élites, rather than nationalist vanguards, wreaked havoc in the societies they pretended to protect from 'the enemies of the people/Volk'.

To my mind, Professor Hermann Giliomee correctly identifies our problem in Sunter's terms as a choice between authoritarian co-optation and endemic violence, and genuine negotiation, stability and economic growth. However, I cannot see an escape from existing authoritarianism through a bi- or multi-communal accommodation of nationalist aspirations.

Instead of the nationalistic self-determination of statutorily defined groups, we rather need the democratic self-determination of free associates to undercut the destructive authoritarian trend and increasingly negative stance of a government that has clearly run out of any viable alternatives.

(Sunday Times, 30 August 1987)

IT MAY BE DANGEROUS, BUT WE'VE JUST GOT TO BUILD THAT NEW ROAD

Lawrence Schlemmer

New roads are very dangerous places to be on in highly polarised political conflicts. Hermann Giliomee's article, 'The Third Way', has been highly controversial and perhaps even wilfully misunderstood.

One of the greatest political sins in South Africa and other deeply divided societies is to challenge the categories in which protagonists place themselves. If one cannot join the protagonists it is safest to be wishy-washy, which Giliomee is most decidedly not. Giliomee argued that, underlying all the obscuring rhetoric, surface ideology and strategic alliances, the real contest in South Africa is between Afrikaner and African nationalism. Both lay claim to effective control over the major instruments of power in the South African territory. Both have a powerful historical momentum. Neither is likely to suffer defeat and collapse save in a war of attrition which will leave no real victors.

African nationalism has survived the most massive onslaught by the State from the fifties onward and will prevail and grow. The National Party has confounded every prediction of imminent collapse and is now as firmly established as ever. Even if it were to collapse or capitulate, a dangerous reserve force of white conservatism and Afrikaner nationalism is waiting in the wings – the CP and its alliances.

Giliomee sees no alternative to the chronic and escalating conflict save for an alternative course – the 'third way'. As I understand it, this route, which he calls 'bi-communalism', involves an acceptance on both sides of the inescapable reality of the opposing force. The deep entrenchment of the opposing power bloc requires resolution akin to an international settlement, probably taking the form of an agreement to share power, a 'pact', hammered out in negotiations.

In Dakar and subsequently, the tendency in the ANC was to reject Giliomee's thesis. As with the National Party, in which Afrikaners have secure, numerically-based control over an alliance with English-speaking whites and therefore can afford to play down Afrikaans identity, the ANC can afford to de-emphasise African nationalism in its alliance with the SA Communist Party and various left-leaning non-African formations.

Its manifest ideology, democratic non-racialism, can never really threaten the reality of the numerical preponderance of the African majority. This allowed the ANC delegates the luxury of rising above the unpleasant realities of nationalisms of any kind. Afrikaner nationalism was described as archaic, chauvinistic and outmoded compared with the universalist and modern ideology of the ANC.

Giliomee, who was crudely misunderstood as pleading the cause of Afrikaner nationalism, long precedes most of the newly enlightened co-

24

delegates to Dakar as an opponent of white domination. There is none so arrogant as the new convert. The basic nature of the South African conflict is complex and could not be finally resolved in Dakar. Aside from the fact that being attacked from both sides is often a compliment to the validity of an argument, one or two uncomfortable questions may be pointers.

If one assumes some future majority-ruled South Africa, could a state president and cabinet be appointed solely on merit and political record without regard to race? Could the leader of the ANC be a white, an Indian or a coloured person? Similarly, could the NP or the CP ever appoint a cabinet with a majority of English-speakers'? Even the most ardent protagonists of non-racial or white solidarity respectively would have to admit that these questions are uncomfortable. In short, I believe that Giliomee is right about the underlying reality of the conflict of nationalisms.

Is a third way possible, however? Is bi-communalism an option? Almost nobody on either side of the conflict is likely to concede this in advance.

For both Afrikaner and African nationalists it will mean a substantial step back from either the power already possessed or the future power taken to be a legitimate right. Hence, the National Party has to continue to try to divide power into 'own' and 'general' affairs so that it can share some power without losing control of the really crucial structures like the *fiscus*, security, major infrastructure, etc.

For the ANC, the prospect of a governing pact with its arch-enemy is hardly compatible with its present mission of a transformation of society and a liberation of the majority from all vestiges of minority rule.

Yet, if a resolution to our conflict is to be found in this century, the following elements will have to be accepted as part of the 'pact':

- Full majority representation in the highest organs of government without reference to any formal constitutional distinction between the powers of communities. Any division of powers making for elements of self-determination for groups would have to be part of the agreement in the pact.
- White leadership in the highest organs of government which is sufficiently trusted and popular to convince the majority of whites that the system is worth participating in. Such leadership will have to have sufficient credibility or leverage in conservative white communities to discourage extra-parliamentary dissidence among groups like the AWB and others, who could become far more dangerous than the 'comrades'.
- A formula, which will inevitably be complex and controversial, to guide the creation of equality of opportunity in our very large civil service without running the very real risk of dissidence in the public sector and a breakdown of administration.
- Sufficient reassurance as regards checks and balances in government, law and order and efficiency of administration to protect what little investor confidence our economy is able to generate.

At the same time economic planning and socio-economic reform will have to address the legitimate needs of the disadvantaged groups in our society so as to create a sense of widening opportunity in the population at large. This is the high road which Giliomee, following Clem Sunter, talks about in his article.

This high road will not emerge, phoenix-like, from the ashes of revolution and probably right-wing counter-revolution. Nor will it emerge from the complicated half-measures of present-day constitutional reform. It can obviously only be the product of high-level political statesmanship in a joint endeavour involving all major mobilised power-groupings in our society – black nationalist groupings, Inkatha, other black movements and the right-wing parties included.

As such, it would be a complete understatement to say that the resolution alluded to is a monumental and, at this stage, remote task requiring attitudes and orientations among the salient actors which are simply not present yet. In the meantime, what South Africa needs most urgently in my view is a movement of leaders across lines of colour, and political parties capable of rising above the divisions of ideology and party politics, performing a bridge-building function. Such a movement will have to accept the realities of all mobilised power-groupings, Afrikaner nationalism and the ANC included.

(Sunday Times, 3 September 1987)

PART II

PAPERS PRESENTED AT THE SYMPOSIUM ON POLITICAL ACCORD IN SOUTH AFRICA: PROBLEMS AND PROSPECTS

Centre for Policy Studies, Johannesburg, January 1988

3

REQUIREMENTS FOR AND POSSIBILITIES OF SUCCESSFUL CONSTITUTIONAL NEGOTIATION IN SOUTH AFRICA

Lawrence Schlemmer

INTRODUCTION

Virtually all actors in the South African political conflict recognise that no ultimate resolution of the situation will be possible without a process of negotiation between the major protagonists. These major contenders are normally taken to include the South African National Party government (obviously), the African National Congress and its base of sympathy within the country (which includes important sections of the United Democratic Front), Inkatha, which although not on a par with the ANC in terms of nation-wide support has a significant regional constituency, the Pan-Africanist Congress (PAC) and the Azapo/National Forum Movement.

Many notions regarding negotiations may have been dangerously over-simplified, both in terms of what is likely to be needed for a successful outcome and as regards the combinations of constituencies and their leaders that should participate. In this brief essay an attempt will be made at exploring some of the major preconditions for a resolution of South Africa's conflict via the debating table.

An important caveat needs to be introduced at the outset. The idea of negotiation as explored here does not necessarily imply some high-key event like a 'national convention'. Indeed, the notion of some kind of 'summit' at which a final grand resolution is achieved would be little more than romantic illusion if it were not incorporated into the aspirations for South Africa of some of the important leaders concerned in the South African conflict. In fact, negotiations are likely to be long drawn-out, stop-start and messy affairs as they usually are in the real world of conflict resolution.

The topic of possible future negotiation will be dealt with under three headings, all interconnected but conceptually distinct:

- the goals of negotiation;

- the conditions for negotiation;
- other indications for the success of the process of negotiation in the short- to medium-term future.

THE GOALS OF NEGOTIATION

Negotiation normally implies that the protagonists are basically in agreement on what is being negotiated. Frequently the topic of negotiation is a variable or set of variables, and the participants will have different objectives as regards the advantages they wish to gain. No matter how widely differentiated the relative advantages may be, the continuum along which these are arranged is usually agreed upon, even if broadly or implicitly. The simplest example is wage negotiation. All parties will agree that the talks are about wages – they will differ only in regard to the relative rewards or costs involved. Similarly, the USA and the Soviet Union both appear to agree that the current nuclear disarmament talks are about types of weapons, their quantities and places of deployment. They are, at this stage, at least in agreement on what the talks are about.

This issue identifies the first major problem in hypothetical future negotiations in South Africa:

'Transformation' versus 'group power-sharing'

It is common knowledge that the goals of negotiation as envisaged by the government are to accomplish a form of power-sharing between formally defined race groups. The principle of group self-determination in regard to 'own affairs' is stated to be non-negotiable at this stage.

The exiled resistance movements, the ANC and the PAC, as well as some of the internal movements loosely aligned to them, on the other hand, are by now firmly committed to the goal of a transformation of internal power relations. During talks with an ANC delegation in Dakar in July 1988[1] it was made quite clear that racially or ethnically based political mobilisation in a hypothetical future dispensation under the ANC would be met with 'liberatory intolerance', as it was put.

Neither view can be taken as mere posturing, likely to be relinquished in an actual process of negotiation. In fact, both stand-points are deeply rooted in white and black political organisation. The National Party government has clearly indicated its determination to protect the framework of group-based power-sharing in rejecting the proposals of the KwaZulu-Natal Indaba, which emphasise voluntary association rather than formal group classification, and also once by criticising constitutional proposals by the Democratic Turnhalle Alliance in Namibia, which are very similar. In both instances the government would have gained considerable credibility, quite apart from the more concrete strategic benefits of potentially being

29

able to strike an accord with Inkatha, had the proposals at least been accepted as a basis for further negotiations.

The political cultures of the resistance movements have for long been powerfully influenced by the model of the decolonisation experience in Africa, in which an overthrow or withdrawal of white rule has become the focal point, with the notion of 'struggle for liberation' as the major basis of mobilisation.

Since the mid-seventies, these features have been reinforced by the adoption by the resistance movements of popular socialist ideals. These have been present in the ANC for a long time, and were generated in the Congress Alliance which included the SA Communist Party. However, whereas the older communist influences were structured around the concept of a two-stage revolution in which socialist goals were not necessarily prominent in the first stage of 'national' liberation, the more recent neo-Marxist influences have had the effect of establishing more immediate priorities for structural change in the economy.

The resistance movements appear to be equally committed to their goal of transformation at this stage. This author's exposure to ANC thinking in the recent intensive debates in Dakar, Senegal, left an almost overwhelming impression of a sense of the historical inevitability of a collapse of the white government. This event is not envisaged as a short-term possibility; indeed there is full acknowledgement (in private conversation) of an extended and bitter armed struggle.

This sobering fact, however, does not seem to incline the members of the movement towards accepting the need for major compromise or seeking intermediate strategies. At times the impression was created of great 're-volutionary patience'. The commitment to a long drawn-out armed struggle is fundamentally supported by a consistent theoretical analysis which emphasises the corrosive effects on the white government of a lack of popular legitimacy, as well as an almost automatic expansion of internal politicisation and resistance. There is a great awareness of a correlation between an awakening consciousness and an expansion of activism and resistance, physically and symbolically spearheaded by the armed struggle.

In this context, political strategies, of which there are a fair range within the organisation, are most explicitly not geared to strategic compromises or trade-offs with white power, but aimed at isolating and weakening the institutions of apartheid society. Thus, apart from the power strategies of sanctions and disinvestment, or the encouragement of strong labour action, a key strategic aim for the ANC has been to discourage participation in government structures in favour of alternative activities at all levels – academic life, community service, welfare, education, etc.

Under these circumstances, little hope can be placed on calls for negotiation between the ANC and the government at this stage, because they would be negotiating on different issues. The almost inevitable result would be that, if negotiations were to commence, strategy on both sides would probably be to negotiate in *bad faith*, each party seeking to manipulate the other in order to attain strategic advantage. The government might conceivably negotiate to secure an end to violence; the ANC to secure the release of political prisoners; and both would probably try to divide the other side in the process.

A further problem at this stage is that the vigorous and public promotion by both sides of their end-goals in possible negotiations tends to have a mutually alienating effect. Viewpoints of the two sides tend to be seen as totally exclusive of each other.

The problem of political asymmetry

The second and related major problem affecting the goals of negotiation is that the government, at this stage at any rate, would negotiate from a position of institutionalised power, with full control over the security system and the administration of communities, whereas the resistance movements would at best be able to use the leverage of informal coercion. Obviously the negotiation would be about power, but in a situation akin to a title-holder defending a title against a contender for the prize: in other words a *zero-sum* power game: 'I win you lose, you win I lose'. Consequently, unless there were some significant cost common to both contenders in not achieving a settlement (see later) there would be no commonality in the exercise – not even calculable rewards like, say, the prize money which two boxers would both receive. This structural asymmetry implies fundamentally incompatible goals, which would, inevitably, result in mutual destruction.

At this stage, therefore, the nature of the expressed goals does not seem to encourage the negotiation process. The situation on both sides is not static, however, and goals may change. The prospects of this occurring are best discussed after considering further requirements for negotiation.

THE BASIC CONDITIONS FOR NEGOTIATION

As implied above, the conditions for negotiation are closely linked to goals: as conditions change, goals may alter. The appropriate conditions for negotiation imply a realisation on both or all sides that something can be gained from settlement, despite sustaining some losses. Upon consideration of such requirements and the concomitant problems, the potential rewards and costs of serious negotiations have to be assessed for both the government and the resistance movements.

Benefit-cost perceptions of negotiation

The rewards on *government side* can be identified hypothetically as the following (in each case problems, costs, impediments and counter-indicating factors will be identified as well):

International respectability and a restoration of status

White South Africans have always prided themselves on being full members of the Western community of nations. Indeed, during the period when General Jan Smuts was a Field Marshall in the British Army and architect of the League of Nations, South African whites, whether they approved of it or not, became accustomed to the idea of an almost élite status in the British Commonwealth.

Like most whites, the South African government has little desire to withdraw into parochialism and obscurity. The Afrikaans media in particular, make much of South Africa's international achievements. At a time when international respect is dwindling rapidly, there is an almost touching excitement when a South African achieves recognition outside our boundaries.

The commencement of a process of negotiation which may lead to a settlement is the one gesture by the South African government which the Western countries would most welcome. As has been the case in Namibia, this factor of Western recognition could probably be a powerful incentive to negotiation.

However, the recent stance adopted by the governments of the USA (the Congress), Canada, Australia and some European countries causes doubt as to whether or not major Western powers would remain impartial in such negotiations. It is one thing to negotiate with the resistance movements, but quite another to negotiate with a phalanx of powerful and apparently partial 'observers' on the other side. This may very well neutralise the expectation of rewards.

Linked to this is the cynical perception of anti-apartheid lobbies in the West that they will only accord legitimacy to a political system in South Africa in which the white government has virtually capitulated. This perception hardly strengthens the urge to negotiate with the major resistance movements.

Avoiding the costs of conflict

The major reason for an interest in negotiation is normally that the costs of not negotiating are perceived to be higher than the costs of concessions made towards reaching a settlement.

The costs to South Africa of continuing political conflict are indeed high. These include a lack of investor confidence and a low level of investment in new productive enterprise (see e.g. comments by ex-Finance Minister OPF Horwood in *The Star*, 18 August 1987), the emigration of highly skilled personnel, complications in industrial relations, high costs of security precautions, and sanctions and disinvestment. There are countless appeals to the government to address these problems through embarking on negotiations towards a resolution of the underlying causes.

The factor of costs as an incentive for major negotiations with the resistance movements is qualified considerably by the following factors:

- There is a widespread perception in government that military and security expenditure in South Africa is low in comparative international terms. Relative military expenditure at roughly 14 per cent of government expenditure in 1987/1988 is below that of some major Western European countries and the USA. (In the USA and West Germany the figure is over 20 per cent.) The police force is small by international standards, at two policemen per 1 000 people. Hence, the costs of containment of conflict are not perceived as critically high – indeed, they could even rise substantially without attaining critical dimensions.

- The economic costs of political conflict are seldom unambiguous, as perceived by politicians. Political conflict or uncertainty is not the only factor producing economic malaise. There are, in any event, thought to be remedies other than a political settlement, such as so-called 'inward industrialization'.

- More importantly, however, there is no absolute certainty that the economy would be stimulated by some form of political debate with resistance movements. Firstly, negotiations are likely to be drawn out, untidy and surrounded by controversy, which will not build confidence. Secondly, if external and internal investors see a prospect of majority rule, particularly if accompanied by socialist tendencies, investor confidence will decline. If a form of balanced power-sharing seems destined to emerge, there will undoubtedly be disaffected factions on the black side, promising more protests and unrest. There is thus a school of thought which holds that political uncertainty will always be with us, and that special strategies are required to stimulate economic activity, politics notwithstanding.

The rewards of negotiation on the side of the *resistance movements* can be identified equally easily, but here again each reward must also be qualified.

The major resistance forces are exiled movements, the members of which, by all accounts, share a collective yearning to return to South Africa in order to participate fully and institutionally in the affairs of their country.

- Like all exiled resistance movements, they have painted themselves to a substantial degree into a revolutionary corner. The mythology of resistance and liberation is strongly geared to the ultimate goal of returning home in triumph to assume the mantle of power. To relinquish the struggle to return to participate in a complex and messy compromise is

33

hardly motivating. Negotiations at this stage could promise little more in terms of reward.

- Exiled movements do not have to carry the costs of not negotiating, unless they are also externally in limbo. A viable external revolutionary movement which has sufficient funds and enjoys substantial recognition *as an organisation*, does not necessarily bear the costs of a long drawn-out conflict. It is usually the non-exiled sympathisers inside the country who pay the price of resistance. In South Africa it is the UDF which has paid the heaviest price of radical opposition. The psychological pressures on the ANC in exile are conceivably much less severe.
- In terms of the mythology of resistance, it can also be argued that struggle is often its own reward. Regrettably world history is replete with models of glorious martyrdom, and as long as recognition is forthcoming from some quarter or another, the commitment to struggle can continue indefinitely.

For these and other reasons, one has to consider whether or not the political conflict in South Africa has inflicted sufficient costs or pain on the formations which are expected to negotiate and which must signal a willingness to negotiate in good faith, with a reasonably open agenda.

It is often argued that a recognition of stalemate in a conflict situation is the key to willingness to negotiate. If, however, a political organisation can remain intact and justify itself, a situation of stalemate can be endured almost indefinitely. Under these circumstances, stalemate in itself is not sufficient to impel political organisations into negotiation.

Furthermore, if the costs of stalemate can be discounted in the expectation that the situation may alter for the better, then the incentive to negotiate may vanish completely. Gambling on an improvement of fortunes has sustained many a conflict.

In South Africa, white politicians who support the idea of the government negotiating away all or much of its power are frequently compelled by a sense of hopelessness, based on an expectation of having to endure conflict and steadily deteriorating material conditions. On the side of the resistance movements, an equivalent perception would be that of increasing losses of trained activists, of diminishing support within the country, and the like.

These may be termed the 'opportunity costs' of political conflict. It is perhaps the most compelling reality of which the major political actors in South Africa have to take account. Yet, one suspects that on both sides of the conflict, there are perceptions of possible future developments which would change the situation to a more beneficial one.

On the side of the resistance movements, and indeed of many black protest movements over the past decades, there is the hope that major powers will intervene to end the struggle in their favour. The sanctions movement, as seen by the ANC, is not to be judged solely in terms of the effectiveness of economic punishment, but as a major strategy to isolate the South African regime from the West, so as to make an active campaign against the South African government by the international community more possible. The hope of major Western nations entering the struggle with strategic aid, and perhaps even more active support, is a compelling dynamic. Even if the prospects seem remote, a South Africa isolated from the West would mean that one or more Eastern bloc powers could intervene actively on the side of the ANC with less chance of US or Western counter-reaction to neutralise the situation.

On the side of the South African government, possibilities are perceived of a major change in the internal situation, which will in time influence external perceptions.

In this regard hopes tend to be pinned on one or more of the following developments:

- a conciliatory leadership emerging among what is perceived to be the 'silent majority' of black South Africans, with whom negotiations within the government's framework will be possible;
- socio-economic reform inducing a change in political consciousness among blacks, which would also allow a more conciliatory attitude emerging in existing movements;
- a swing of sympathies in Western public opinion, based on the recognition that unqualified universal franchise in South Africa could carry the risks of an anti-democratic outcome, or socialism, with economic effects similar to those elsewhere in independent Africa.

None of the above possibilities can be ruled out completely, no matter how remote some may seem. Politicians *par excellence* are risk-takers, and gambling on a 'turn of fate' is nothing new in history. Living in hope is one way of avoiding the harsh realities of the need to compromise.

In general, therefore, the issue of rewards versus costs of a continuing conflict does not necessarily induce the kind of conditions which would bring the prospect of negotiations any nearer.

The disabilities of leadership without organised constituencies

Negotiations presuppose not only the leaders' willingness to compromise but also their authority to accept compromises which are binding upon and acceptable to their followers or constituencies. This authority is contained in the mandate to negotiate which the leader has received from his followers. This in turn requires that such a leader is chosen, by vote or popular acclaim, by an organised constituency.

Where this mandate is lacking, a 'representative' in negotiations will be at a severe disadvantage. He or she will not know the parameters within which concessions can be made and will not be able to convene meetings at short notice within the constituency to find out whether or not particular compromises will be endorsed.

Among the black opposition and resistance movements it is virtually only the trade union movement and Inkatha which are sufficiently organised to present their 'people's mandate'. The civic associations are locally based and are noted for not holding regular meetings of organised and enrolled adherents. The powerful youth movements are similarly disadvantaged. The exiled resistance movements, by definition, do not have organised constituencies, although they have great popular support. The formally elected black town councillors in most cases have been voted in by very small percentages of township residents. Religious leaders more often than not do not have a political mandate from the members of their churches.

Apart from the trade unions and Inkatha, the internal black leadership, therefore, is largely comprised of 'spokesmen' for particular, usually popular, points of view. The expression of such viewpoints may carry overwhelming endorsement, but the problems relating to mandates for compromises and concessions remain. How does a religious leader who is also a political spokesman know what compromises he or she can make? Uncertainty in this regard could well cause the spokesperson to be less flexible than a constituency leader would be.

The solution to the problem lies both with the government and with black leadership. The government has to make sure that it does not inhibit or prevent potentially constructive and peaceful organisations from growing and becoming sufficiently coherent to negotiate. Black spokesmen would do well to recognise that their ultimate challenge before negotiations is to mobilise in such a way as to acquire the visible support of organised constituencies.

OTHER FACTORS RELEVANT TO THE SUCCESS OF NEGOTIATIONS IN THE SHORT- TO MEDIUM-TERM FUTURE

The issues raised in previous sections are the larger contextual variables bearing upon the prospects for negotiation. There are, however, other factors of a lesser significance when taken singly, but which in combination can be a major set of either impediments or incentives to the commencement of negotiation.

The quality of South African political rhetoric

One of the 'process' requirements in conflict resolution is that of avoiding rhetoric and posturing which may discourage participants on the other side of the negotiating table. Conflict resolution is usually facilitated where rhetoric on both sides is deliberately tempered to sound accommodating, conciliatory, inviting and even perhaps to some extent, repentant. This is extremely problematic in the South African situation.

Government spokesmen tend to reassure more conservative elements both inside the National Party and in the right-wing opposition groups that negotiation across colour lines is not the beginning of a sell-out of white interests. Hence one of the political objectives which is frequently articulated in the media is 'white self-determination', couched in fairly stark terms.

This type of rhetoric is received by black opposition movements within the context of a history of racial discrimination. It is impossible for them to disentangle the concept of white autonomy from white 'baasskap' or racial segregation: hence the perception that the government's framework for talks will be limiting in the extreme.

Black opposition movements and resistance groupings have had to endure painful setbacks and severe constraints in their political programmes. Partly in order to maintain their own morale, and partly in response to frustration, their rhetoric has tended to become somewhat highly charged. Consider the following quotes from prominent black leaders, by way of example:

The Reverend Alan Boesak has argued: '(The future) ... can't be the capitalism that oppresses people here ... where only the élite benefit from the wealth and it never reaches the people.'[2]

Archbishop Tutu says: 'Capitalism and the free-enterprise system – it is unfreedom, it is morally repulsive.'[3]

Winnie Mandela is more direct: 'It is not us, but the white man, who should be thinking of how he will fit into our future society. It is his problem. There he sits ... oppressing us for all these generations and now we must [are called upon to] worry about the protection of minority rights, and of his property and culture.'[4]

Such sentiments are, of course, completely justified from the perspective of black protest. They are, however, as threatening to whites as 'white self-determination' is to blacks. The result is a climate inimical to negotiation.

Mistrust, and the need for an agenda

A keynote feature of our society is mutual alienation across race lines, brought about by centuries of domination and social segregation.

It is probably true to say that the perception among most black movements is that the government wishes to 'negotiate' in order to divide, confuse and co-opt its opposition. On government side there is probably a perception that the external resistance movements in particular wish to negotiate only about the surrender of power by government.

There have been many calls on government to produce at least a 'statement of intent' regarding negotiations, and preferably an agenda. The government, for justifiable reasons, considers that if it were to declare its negotiating position in advance, it would either be seen as top-down prescription or it would discourage participation in negotiations.

The fact that negotiating frameworks are so far apart (see earlier) poses a serious problem for the government, since it wishes to negotiate with black leaders and movements which thus far have been more than reluctant to come forward, at least publicly. One way out of this impasse is suggested below.

The need for objective agencies to facilitate negotiation

The problem raised above cannot be resolved by the South African government. Should it determine an agenda, it would do so from a position of power and it would obviously reveal its hand. There seems to be little option, as far as internal negotiations are concerned, but for an impartial agency to be established through which negotiation can be facilitated and arranged.

The following options seem worthy of consideration. A Supreme Court judge could be appointed to lead a negotiating commission, with participation in negotiations by all parties, and not by the government itself but by the National Party. This commission could determine the agenda after preliminary 'talks about talks'. An alternative to a judicial commission could be an international 'group', approved by all sides. The process of approval would be very problematic, however. Another variant on this theme would be the appointment of two prominent South Africans, one black and one white, as joint chairmen of a negotiating initiative.

The need for bridging initiatives

A survey of all the problems mentioned in previous sections tends to reinforce the impression that conditions in South Africa may not yet be ripe for a process of negotiation to commence. This is a depressing thought, particularly since the conditions suitable for negotiation would then only be established after much more pain and destruction has been inflicted on the society. This is clearly not a tenable or moral conclusion for people concerned about a peaceful resolution of South Africa's conflict.

For this reason it is essential for initiatives to commence or to be encouraged at levels or in regions of the society where the frameworks for negotiation of the major actors are more compatible than at the national level. One has in mind here negotiation-based initiatives aimed at interim power-sharing arrangements either at local authority level or in specified regions of the country. The KwaZulu-Natal initiative is one major example but since it has been so well publicised, it is unnecessary to discuss it here. Other possibilities deserve exploration.

One such possibility frequently mooted is that of local-level negotiations on specific community problems, involving leaders and movements currently reluctant to work within the system. Private sector organisations, after demonstrating impartiality and the willingness to take local community aspirations seriously, may be able to form working alliances with such organisations. One problem would remain of how to engage the authorities in such negotiations in a way which would not be seen as symbolically inappropriate by the community.

The Regional Services Councils (RSCs), operating at metropolitan and regional levels, are administrative frameworks within which bulk services are supplied to white and black areas within the region, with a new fiscal base to fund the services. Multiracial councils are responsible for the planning and implementation of policy, based on a formula which gives richer and better developed local authorities greater numerical representation than less-developed black local authorities. The RSCs are controversial not only because of this fact but also because, by drawing representation from racially segregated local areas, they reinforce the principle of residential and municipal segregation along lines of race. Yet, in terms of the legislation, they provide for the bulk of expenditure to go to the black (or less-developed) local authorities. The first (1987/88) budget speech of the chairman of the Central Witwatersrand Council seemed to indicate that full effect will be given to this provision.

While they have been rejected thus far by most (but not all) significant local black leadership, the RSCs may be a starting-point for the type of 'bridging' exercise that is referred to above. The following is merely an illustration of what could occur.

If the participants in a Regional Services Council were to try to overcome their lack of legitimacy in black areas, they could for example appoint a sub-committee to draw wider participation from all communities into a 'forum' which in the first instance would be informal and advisory, but which could negotiate its composition and its priorities. This 'forum' need not be closely associated with the RSC in the initial stages, and could be a link to the private sector negotiating 'alliance' referred to above.

Existing legislation allows local authorities to cooperate (on a so-called 'agency' basis) across a wider range of activities than merely the supply of bulk services. Through this mechanism a range of priorities could be addressed, initially on a basis of informal inter-authority cooperation, with the (informal) approval and facilitation of the official Regional Services Council.

If all these inputs could be carefully orchestrated, a 'local option' involving informal power-sharing could emerge, which would not only have concrete benefits for local communities, but which would be a demonstration of balanced power-sharing in action. If in addition, the official RSC, with its formal leverage, were to campaign for a change in legislation to formalise a more acceptable power-sharing arrangement, a local dispensation could emerge involving a model of negotiated power-sharing for other regions and for the country as a whole. This is merely an example of an interim process which could in the longer run facilitate a wider thrust towards power-sharing in the society. The multilateral approach may sound clumsy but may be necessary to overcome the existing hostility and alienation.

The analysis given in this chapter has been very broad, but it suggests nonetheless that a negotiated peace in South Africa, although still possible, will have no easy passage. The existing impediments are forbidding enough, let alone the enormous problems which are likely to emerge when the actual process commences.

In this situation, it behoves all South Africans at all levels to communicate across lines of race and power as much as possible, in order to improve the climate for the negotiated settlement which must ultimately take place. Given the manifest and costly stalemate in the society, it is also perhaps appropriate that all lesser opportunities be grasped and utilised, since success at this level will facilitate more comprehensive negotiations in the medium term.

NOTES
[1] The author attended the Dakar talks as an invited speaker.
[2] Interview with Allan Boesak, in Neuhaus, R J, *Dispensations: The future of South Africa as South Africans see it*, Grand Rapids, Michigan: Eerdmans, 1986.
[3] Interview with Archbishop Tutu, in Neuhaus, op. cit.
[4] Mandela, W, *Part of my soul*, London: Penguin, 1986.

4

THE GOVERNMENT'S FRAMEWORK FOR CONSTITUTIONAL CHANGE AND NEGOTIATION

Stoffel van der Merwe

It should be clear to all that the South African government is not proceeding with its programme of constitutional change aimlessly or without a fairly clear framework of what it has in mind for the future.

On the one hand the government, mindful of the fact that a commitment to a particular blueprint for a future political system would be counter-productive by being one-sided, tries to keep the agenda for future change and negotiations as open as possible. On the other hand, going into a reform process without having specific goals would be highly irresponsible. The framework outlined below gives some direction to the process.

The first principle of the framework is that all citizens must share in political decision-making on an equal basis. By citizens we mean also those black people who had previously lost their South African citizenship in favour of citizenship of one of the self-governing territories or the independent states, provided that they live within the boundaries of the Republic of South Africa (but excluding the TBVC states). This means that every person should eventually have a vote on all the levels of government.

However, it needs to be noted that there is no democracy of significance in the world which follows a simple system of 'one man one vote'. The constituency system in Britain as well as that of the House of Lords, through which government with a minority of popular votes is sometimes put into power, deviates slightly from the simple 'one man one vote' principle. This is also the case with the Senate in the United States, the members of which are not elected on a proportional basis but on that of one state two senators, regardless of the number of inhabitants of the particular state. The same principle applies to countries such as France and Germany.

These deviations are made to accommodate the cultural and historical peculiarities of each country. What we should therefore do in South Africa is to develop a system in which the principle of one man one vote is adapted in such a way as to make provision for the particular circumstances of South African society – while maintaining the basic principle.

This brings us to the second consideration in the government's framework for the future, i.e. the principle that no single group should be able to dominate other groups or the entire political system.

One could say that this principle is so basic to democracy that it hardly needs mentioning. However, the undifferentiated application of the 'one man one vote' principle in several African states did in fact lead to one group dominating the entire system to the detriment of other groups. When this happens, the vote of the minority groups is reduced to mere symbol and theory, as is the case in one-party states.

If one wants to establish a real democracy, therefore, care must be taken to construct the system in such a way that the vote of all members of all groups remains a real vote.

The third consideration is that peace and stability should be maintained, not only in the future political system, but also during the process leading up to the development and establishment of such a system.

This rules out the principle of establishing a democracy through a process of violent revolution. Democracy is essentially a system for the peaceful resolution of political disputes. One talks, votes, goes to court and applies all sorts of peaceful mechanisms – but one never resorts to violence. If violence is legitimated as the means through which a new system is established, it becomes very difficult to prevent violence being used in future political actions.

In fact, no violent revolution in history has ever brought democracy in its wake. Revolutions were generally followed by lengthy periods of violent dictatorships, and democracy had to emerge anew after long struggles. Good examples are the French, Russian, and Iranian revolutions.

It therefore becomes an overriding consideration to maintain minimum standards of law and order during the process leading up to the establishment of a democracy.

A fourth consideration is that political or constitutional reform cannot develop in isolation. It needs to be accompanied and underscored by development and reform on the social and economic fronts. Giving people a full vote in the central government without ensuring that the existing social and economic conditions are such that the demands of the newly enfranchised electorate can be met, is courting disaster, and eventually only serves to discredit the very idea of democracy. Even in established democracies the governments from time to time need to take actions contrary to demands from the electorate. In a newly established democracy, especially one which was established after a violent struggle, it becomes much more difficult for the government to resist exorbitant demands without resorting to undemocratic solutions such as the one-party state or even a dictatorship.

A fifth parameter of the government's framework for constitutional change is the principle of decentralisation of decision-making, as far as possible. This will allow communities in a multicultural environment to take decisions according to their own norms and values, on as many issues as possible. Unfortunately it is not always possible in a changing environment to give effect to this principle as quickly as is desirable. The reasons for this are twofold.

Firstly, in the absence of a clear new structure for society, everything tends to become politicised so that a minor incident can have nationwide or indeed worldwide repercussions. It is therefore necessary for the central government to maintain some degree of control until such time as the new structure of society has been well established and such issues become de-politicised.

Secondly, it is often necessary to reconstruct certain functions in a different way, which means that they first have to be centralised, away from the existing localities, reconstructed, and then decentralised in a different form. The recent changes at second and third level of government in South Africa are a good example in this regard.

Inherent in these circumstances is the danger that power may be centralised – with good intentions – and left there. The commitment of the government to the principle of decentralisation has to be strong indeed.

In practice, decentralisation is effected by creating decentralised structures but with (temporary) centralised control. The centralised control can then be relinquished gradually as these structures are developed for satisfactory decision-taking and as the issues become less politicised, as mentioned above.

Another part of the government's framework is the maintaining of Christian values and civilised norms. This may seem imperious in view of the fact that non-Christian religions also exist in South Africa, although the vast majority of people in South Africa profess to be of a Christian faith. It should also be noted that the maintaining of Christian values does not imply that a Christian religion will be established as the state religion. And surely nobody could oppose the idea of civilised norms. One may refer to democracy and the abhorrence of violence as one of the major civilised norms.

The seventh parameter of government policy is an economy based on the protection of private enterprise. This does not entail full 'capitalism' in its classic sense (which has in any case never existed in South Africa) but the creation of circumstances within which each individual can apply his entrepreneurial skills to the best possible advantage. It has been proved over and again that an economy based on private enterprise in the end creates the most wealth for all members of that society.

At the same time of course, known evils of capitalism such as monopolies should be kept under control. The commitment of the government to this goal is clearly visible in its drive for deregulation and privatisation, its vigorous support for the development of small businesses through the Small Business Development Corporation and its actions through the Competitions Board.

The theoretical and emotional attraction of socialism as an economic system is obvious when a large portion of the population has experienced a disadvantaged economic position, as is the case in South Africa. The traps inherent in socialism have, however, been amply illustrated in the rest of Africa and elsewhere. The challenge is for the government, the private sector, and indeed everybody in South Africa, to make a success of the system of private enterprise and create an economy which will be to the advantage of all.

As has been stated, a new political, social and economic system for South Africa has to be created through a process of negotiation. Without this process it would be very difficult to create a system which would really meet the needs of our diverse population or which would muster sufficient support.

Now, with whom should the government negotiate in this regard? The simple answer is: with all leaders who are desirous of creating a peaceful and democratic future for South Africa through a process of peaceful and negotiated change.

This excludes one important group of people, i.e. those who are committed to a process of revolutionary and violent change. It has been proved throughout world history that revolutions are unpredictable and seldom, if ever, reach their initial aims. More often than not the fruits of revolution are aimless destruction of valuable human and physical assets and a lapse into dictatorship which can only be overcome through a tedious and lengthy process of reconstruction. Democracy very seldom follows in the footsteps of revolution.

On the other hand, the government has opened up an avenue for peaceful negotiation by its commitment to an assured future for all South Africans, including political participation for all at all levels.

One important impediment to the process of negotiated reform is the large degree of mistrust which exists due to historical and other factors, among the various groups in South Africa. This is of course exaggerated by the continuous misinterpretation of the motives of the government by people and organisations who do not wish to see its reform programme succeed because of their own commitment to revolutionary change.

Despite considerable pressure and despite having paid a heavy price in terms of loss of support at the polls, the government has steadfastly kept to its course of reform.

The framework outlined above should provide ample evidence of the government's intentions regarding a future political system, and warrants serious attention by all parties interested in the future of South Africa.

5

THE NATIONAL PARTY AND THE KWA-NATAL INDABA

P J Steenkamp

INTRODUCTION

The Natal/Kwazulu region features in many schemes devised in opposition to government thinking. On the one hand, part of this province – the predominantly Zulu part of it – is to be included in the 'Boerestaat', as proposed by the adherents of certain movements committed to the ideal of an exclusively white homeland. On the other hand, there exists a school of thought which proposes that the entire region is to be dealt with as a political entity, in terms of structures that would effectively consolidate KwaZulu to include Natal and all its peoples – as an appendage to KwaZulu.

Efforts in the latter direction commenced with the Lombard Report sponsored by the Sugar Association and aimed at kindling alternatives to government policy for the region. It stressed the economic interdependence of KwaZulu and Natal. The subsequent Buthelezi Commission based its approach on the economic interdependence mentioned above. The most recent exercise in providing a constitutional framework treating the region as an economic and political entity, was the Kwa-Natal Indaba.

The National Party acknowledges the economic interdependence of KwaZulu and Natal – as it acknowledges a similar interdependence among all sectors of the Southern African community, including the independent and self-governing territories and even our northern neighbours. The irrecusable existence of these different political units in what could be seen as an economic whole bears testimony to the nature of the challenge facing us: it is more than merely economic; it is political with *all* that that entails. This task is a daunting one which cannot be dealt with in a unilateral or even dictatorial fashion (although such may be the methods prevailing in Africa) as that invariably spells disaster – politically as well as economically.

The National Party, therefore, welcomed the opportunity afforded all the Indaba participants to analyse the political problems and aspirations of the peoples of KwaZulu and Natal; an opportunity which could, amongst other things, create a clearer perception of the political complexities facing a responsible government in this country. Furthermore, the NP was committed to taking fair cognisance of any proposals made at the Indaba.

It would have been naive in the extreme, however, for the politically seasoned in the NP to believe that the result would dovetail (to put it generously) with matured government perceptions and criteria, for the following reasons:

- The vast majority of the participants and participating organisations had little or no political experience and no political mandate whatsoever.
- All the political parties present were either vehemently opposed to NP policy or at least in concert verbally against it; the Indaba was their opportunity to fabricate an alternative.

The wise could have predicted fairly accurately the gist of the final result. Hence for the NP of Natal to have participated in such a venture, composed in such an *ad hoc* fashion, would have been at best an exercise in futility. The observer status assumed by the NP of Natal was, nonetheless, recognition of the value of a continuing political debate.

CRITIQUE OF THE INDABA PROPOSALS

In a brief summary of the National Party's apprehensions about the proposed constitution it is appropriate to let senior NP politicians speak for themselves.

On the economic shortcomings of the model, the Deputy Minister of Economic Affairs and Technology, George Bartlett, expressed himself as follows:[1] 'Existing government expenditure in the region exceeds income – that is of all taxes – by something like 22 per cent, the shortfall being met by the central government. This does not include the police force, the justice department and the regional defence expenditure which are proposed by the Indaba and which should be borne by the Natal-KwaZulu region. The Bill of Rights demands equalisation of education and health facilities within one year. To do this would bankrupt Natal overnight.'

The Durban Chamber of Commerce became concerned about these economic implications. I quote from a report headed 'Economic realities and reform' in the Durban Metropolitan Chamber of Commerce's Information Digest of 24 January 1987: 'The Chamber is concerned, however, regarding the cost implications of removing discriminatory legislation and has repeatedly stressed that these implications must be recognised so that unobtainable objectives are not set nor unachievable expectations created. Failure to do this would lead to such strains being placed on the Natal economy that a catch-22 situation could arise in which the very urgency with which political reform is tackled, makes it impossible to achieve.'

It is indeed ironic, and a little sad, that even those who played an active part in constituting the Indaba and footed the bill, i.e. commerce and industry, felt a bit let down by the outcome!

The consequences of the Indaba proposals for education in the province are indeed far-reaching – as explained by Minister Stoffel Botha.[2] 'According to the Bill of Rights, financial parity in schools has to be achieved in one year. An equal division of finances is therefore being recommended. I have been informed that this implies that expenditure on white education will have to be curtailed by 75 per cent. This will of course entail a drastic lowering of standards. For the rest, qualified teachers will be distributed to where their services are required the most.' The education committee therefore found as follows, and I quote: 'One of the major areas for further work is to move many hundreds of qualified teachers from those schools where they currently work, to deprived areas.'

The committee consequently planned, and I quote further: '… an orientation period in which teachers can be confronted with the realities of schools different from those with which they are familiar.'

Apart from the disruption of the teaching profession, everyone in Class 1 would be provided with free education. In this regard the Indaba found, and I quote: 'This would mean a growth in pupil numbers on an explosive basis as Zimbabwe had on Independence – that is 50 per cent. In this case there would be a desperate need to explore the same range of possibilities as that country used – platoon classes, hot seat classes, imports of teachers …'

The NP is adamant that children shall not be used as the storm-troopers of political change. We do not believe that shortcomings can be addressed by wrecking that which has already been achieved. Nor do we believe that political stability in South Africa will be enhanced by undermining the existing self-determination regarding the education of their children, enjoyed by the various population groups.

Our criticism of the composition and functioning of the legislature derives from observing the realities of Africa – and the world, for that matter. These realities have been studied and aptly summarised by the celebrated constitutional expert, Prof. Lijphart, in his treatise on power-sharing in South Africa:[3] 'The comparative empirical evidence on the strength and persistance of ethnicity is overwhelming. In South Africa it is therefore highly probable – nay, virtually certain – that the ethnic factor will reassert itself under conditions of free association and open electoral competition.'

The implications of this for Natal become clear if one considers the ethnic composition of the province: 80 per cent Zulu, 10 per cent Indian, 8 per cent white and 2 per cent coloured.

Lijphart's conviction that it is wishful thinking to hope for a lasting natural balance of power between minorities on the one hand and the majority on the other simply cannot be dismissed. He puts it as follows: 'The majority segment will always be tempted to revert to majoritarian methods. In Northern Ireland a Protestant majority twice as large as the Catholic minority was the underlying cause for the failure of the brief power-sharing experiment in 1972, and it continues to be the biggest ob-

47

stacle to the efforts of the British government to find a solution by means of a power-sharing executive and proportional representation. Similarly, the principal cause of the collapse of the Cypriot consociation in 1963 was the four-to-one population imbalance in favour of the Greek Cypriots.'

In Natal we have a four-to-one population imbalance in favour of the Zulus ...

The implications of the fact that the Indaba's First Chamber and the cabinet will be dominated by Zulus and that they likewise will have a major share in the Second Chamber as well as in standing committees[4] – apart from being able to pass all financial bills on their own – have been argued in detail and *ad nauseum* in the minority report and elsewhere.[5] I shall present the conclusions as expressed by some NP cabinet ministers.

On 30 November 1986, shortly after the premature termination of the Indaba, the Natal leader of the NP, Stoffel Botha, issued the following statement: 'Negotiated structures must make provision for equal power-sharing without the domination of any group by another. The National Party of Natal is convinced that the model agreed upon by the Indaba by majority vote, does not satisfy these criteria and hence cannot associate itself with this model.'

The hysterical reaction to this statement bears testimony to the belief in certain quarters that the NP had been painted into an embarrassing corner and hence was expected to resort to double talk characterised by evasion and vagueness.

Efforts to isolate Mr Botha's views from those of his cabinet colleagues also failed. Minister Chris Heunis put paid to that by a Press statement on 27 November 1987: 'There is a fundamental difference between minority protection in a majority model and efficient group participation on the basis of power-sharing. The Indaba model adopts the former. That is why the majority party will be dominant in all institutions, with provision only being made for mechanisms by which minorities can retard majority opinion or, when the cultural interests of a group are involved, make use of the courts to stop the process ... In accordance with the latter approach, groups on the other hand, have an equal say and take joint decisions on a basis in accordance with which numbers are not decisive. Each group, therefore, has an effective veto on all matters, and hence a single group cannot dominate the others.'

He concluded: 'It is clear that my colleague, the leader of the National Party of Natal, and I are in absolute accord about deficiencies in the Indaba proposals and that there definitely exists no difference of opinion between us, as hinted in recent Press reports. It is also clear to me that one of the lessons of the Indaba is that only government institutions, including political parties and groupings, should play the final role in any constitutional reform, and not people who have no power-base or public responsibility.'

There have also been hints to the effect that some officials in the Department of Constitutional Development and Planning are rather inclined towards the Indaba proposals. It is as well to remember that the tail seldom wags the dog.

A penetrating analysis of the Indaba proposals reveals that Prof Thomashausen's findings are most appropriate to this model.[6] 'Ethnic minorities will never be a threat or a useful clientele in democratic terms. They will, therefore, be forced to seek protection of their interests through means of pressure other than the vote. Forced into a potential conflict with democratic majority rule, the isolated, i.e. ethnically or otherwise segregated, minority will continuously be neglected.'

The minority that will sacrifice most in terms of self-determination is the Indians. They have their power-base in Natal. It will be destroyed; hence their rather lukewarm approach to the Indaba. Whites are equally unimpressed: the results of the recent election sank the Indaba alliance convincingly.

A LOST OPPORTUNITY

Now, more than a year after the Indaba, some Indaba protagonists still act as if we are on the way to fairyland via the Indaba. It would be more realistic to perceive the Indaba proposals as another lost opportunity in South African politics.

What went wrong?

The first failure was the distortion of the Indaba point of departure which stipulated that legislation based on racial discrimination was unacceptable. This was promptly and deliberately interpreted to mean that any reference to and recognition of race in the proposals would be taboo. This hypersensitivity (race is after all a given and not a crime) resulted in amazing, and even amusing, footwork from the Indaba intellectuals:

(a) Whites were carefully split into English and Afrikaners to save the Second Chamber from a race tag – in spite of the fact that never in history were these two groups politically more united than at present (more so than the Zulus!).

(b) No voters' rolls for the various groups composing the Second House could be afforded; that would smack of the Population Registration Act. (This should result in some interesting episodes during elections!)

One appreciates the aversion to racial discrimination and can be adamant that all races and groups should be afforded a place in the political sun. Equating 'distinction' with 'discrimination' will, however, not bring this about but will merely ensure that the numerically superior race will dominate, à la Lijphart.

I would suggest that 'black nationalism' might be merely a euphemism for black racism – as manifested in Africanisation programmes! The pre-independence preoccupation of African liberation movements with the abolition of offensive racially based constitutions merely serves to give their own race complete control, after which the strongest black ethnic group takes over. Too often human dignity and democratic sentiments are forgotten after having served their purpose! In South Africa such an approach would be fatal to *all* of us.

Chris Heunis said it all in Parliament:[7] 'I want to put it clearly that this country has a dangerous reality as far as constitutional and political solutions are concerned. We can easily talk about a non-ethnic and non-racial South Africa; we can conduct the most attractive theoretical discussions about it. No constitution of this country can, however, do away with the fact of multi-ethnicity and multiracialism. A system that does not accommodate this characteristic of our society has no hope of maintaining democracy.'

By 'accommodating' we do not mean a symbolic recognition of these facts à la the Indaba, but a system that recognises the right to proper self-determination of the various population groups that compete for power – irrespective of their numerical strength. Students of politics would do well to take note of this fact, irrespective of their measure of predisposition towards Western-style democracy.

The second and most important failure of the Indaba was that it did not heed the directives of the State President and of Chief Buthelezi on power-sharing.

As for the State President:[8] 'Consultation and negotiation must take place on the premise that a suitable constitutional dispensation for the Republic must meet the requirements, at every level of government, of protection and self-determination of minority groups, power-sharing among groups in respect of common affairs and the prevention of domination by any group of the others.'

In his declaration of intent, submitted to various heads of state, Chief Buthelezi put it succinctly:[9] 'We need to share power in such a way that no one group can dictate to any other group how to express its own self-determination.' He continued: 'It is my carefully considered judgement that all black leaders committed to the politics of negotiation could sell such a declaration of intent to their supporters, and I am totally convinced that Mr PW Botha could in fact sell this declaration of intent.'

Indeed, there can be no compromise on these guide-lines as spelled out by the State President and the Chief Minister of KwaZulu. It is the only realistic and honourable course.

The Indaba accepted Chief Buthelezi's Declaration of Intent unanimously – and then conveniently shelved it. This is the tragedy. It opted, instead, for a system diametrically opposed to the guide-lines of these two men. It adopted a majoritarian model, because, in the words of Dr Oscar Dhlomo,

Secretary-General of Inkatha:[10] 'A political solution will have to recognise the legitimate rights of the majority to exercise political power commensurate with their numerical strength.'

At least we are getting closer to the truth all the time!

Dr Dhlomo is also Chairman of the Joint Executive Authority (JEA) in Natal which operates according to the non-dominating, power-sharing principles envisaged by the State President and the Chief Minister of KwaZulu. It is understood, however, that the JEA is to be used as the launching pad for the Indaba proposals ... This may indeed contribute to even greater conflict because the majoritarian approach is a stumbling-block to the power-sharing ideal of PW Botha and Mangosuthu Buthelezi.

If a system of power-sharing without group domination should fail in this country, the theory of total partition would be enhanced out of all proportion to its relevance; let there be no illusions about this.

In conclusion: the impression created by white liberals and their bigoted cohorts at the Indaba, as well as by certain industrialists, namely that whites and other minorities are ready to capitulate, raised unrealistic expectations and resulted in political opportunism and greed: and an opportunity for meaningful discussion was lost. Furthermore, constitutional reform is currently being delayed by a preoccupation with efforts to raise the Indaba phoenix from the ashes.

The important question is whether Inkatha indeed believes in the non-domination power-sharing principles as formulated by its president, Chief Buthelezi, or whether it has opted for the majoritarian approach espoused by its secretary-general. The answer to this question will determine the nature and extent of Inkatha's involvement in a future constitutional dispensation for South Africa.

NOTES

[1] *Hansard,* January 1987, col 156.
[2] *Hansard,* January 1987, col 189.
[3] A Lijphart, Power-sharing in South Africa, Policy Papers in International Affairs No 24, University of California, Berkeley, 1985.
[4] KwaZulu Natal Indaba: Constitutional Proposals and Memoranda, January 1987.
[5] P J Steenkamp, *Indicator Project South Africa: New Frontiers – The KwaZulu Natal Debates,* p 45, October 1987, University of Natal.
[6] E A M Thomashausen, *The Comparative and International Law Journal of Southern Africa,* November 1985, p 313.
[7] *Hansard,* June 1987, col 1148.
[8] *Hansard,* January 1987, col 19.
[9] Policy speech by the Chief Minister of KwaZulu, March 1986.
[10] O A Dhlomo, *Indicator Project South Africa: New Frontiers – The KwaZulu Natal Debates,* p 42, October 1987, University of Natal.

6

THE SCOPE OF REGIME SUPPORT: A CASE STUDY

Jannie Gagiano

'We aim at widening the crack in the white wall. We want to neutralise some of the elements who under normal circumstances would be our enemies ... We are not suggesting that the white businessmen and Afrikaner intellectuals are our temporary allies; but we do suggest that if we can manage it, let us detach them from the most reactionary clique, the Botha regime.'[1]

Those who seek the signs of breakdown in the hegemony of the Afrikaner-based regime in South Africa have been looking at the developments surrounding the Independent Movement which contested seats against the ruling National Party during the general election in 1987. The major figures that came to be associated with this movement all had impeccable Nationalist political credentials and many of them had been leading lights in laying the ideological groundwork for the reformist strategies deployed by the regime in the early eighties.

Denis Worrall, who took on the Minister of Constitutional Development and Planning, Chris Heunis, in the Helderberg constituency had been the chairman of the Constitutional Committee of the President's Council investigating a constitutional alternative for the South African polity, and as the South African ambassador to Britain was highly regarded in government circles as a spirited defender of the reformist policies of the regime.

Wynand Malan, another member of the now fractured Independent troika (Esther Lategan, a Stellenbosch businesswoman with an irreproachable Afrikaner Nationalist pedigree was the third) used to be regarded as a leading figure among a group of *verligte* Afrikaner Nationalists who could keep the National Party attractive to the young, urban, middle-class professionals and thereby secure their continued support for government plans to safeguard the regime.

Almost half of the 28 Stellenbosch academics who issued a statement attacking some of the fundamental principles and practices of government policy (e.g. the Group Areas Act, the statutory definition of groups on a racial basis, the tricameral parliament, the Separate Amenities Act) are members of the Afrikaner 'Broederbond' and almost all are influential in the community and certain government circles. A number of them were insiders in the decision-making process of government itself.

During the election campaign the Independent candidates, wary of the still salient ethnic factor in white politics and mindful of the lack of success the ideologically liberal Progressive Federal Party has had in attracting Afrikaners to its ranks, projected itself as a home for Afrikaners to the left of the National Party. They reasoned that the only way to liberalise the polity was by goading the Afrikaner-based National Party into a more vigorous pursuit of its reformist goals through the anticipated loss of support to the Independents if they failed to do so.

The Independents' project was embraced by all the major contenders within the bounds of the polity who were seeking to liberalise the political regime. Thus the Inkatha movement gave its blessing and offered its Indaba proposals as a guide-line to a future dispensation, the Labour Party in the House of Representatives promised support, the English-speaking Press reacted enthusiastically, and the official opposition in the House of Assembly, the PFP, left the field free for the Independent candidates in the election by electing not to put up candidates in those constituencies and urging their supporters to vote for the new hopefuls. A number of big businessmen weighed in with substantial financial contributions and there was talk of some 30 National Party Members of Parliament defecting to the new movement after the election.

The Independent project met with moderate success. Malan retained the seat he won as a Nationalist in 1981, Lategan polled some 1 500 votes more in Stellenbosch than any opposition party has managed since the fifties and Worrall came within a whisker of beating the senior cabinet minister and leader of the Cape National Party, Chris Heunis, in the Helderberg constituency.

Do these events signal the onset of a process of élite fragmentation in the Afrikaner political community? This community together with right-wing forces, could fracture élite consensus to the point where it must fail to sustain the hegemony of the regime and thereby render it vulnerable to the revolutionary challenge emerging from nationalist and populist forces in the black communities. Is it, furthermore, conceivable that the formations establishing themselves to the left of the National Party in white politics will be willing partners in a coalition on revolutionary challengers to the Botha regime?

One of the empirical indicators of élite dissension in the Afrikaner political community is the defections from the ranks of the National Party. The party, however, no longer constitutes a consensus underpinning the regime. It has been supplanted by the State itself. Under the Botha administration and certainly since the inauguration of the tricameral parliamentary system, principal governmental decision-making has moved out of Parliament and into the hands of bureaucratic and technocratic élites, with an important influence accorded the security establishment. The major mediating institutions between the Afrikaner political community and the

State such as the churches, the Afrikaner 'Broederbond' and the National Party have correspondingly lost ground as organisational loci of political power in the system. Bolstered by a practically unfettered access to the resources of the State, the government has progressively established an autonomy *vis à vis* the community institutions of Afrikanerdom. Thus the pattern of the relationship between the Afrikaner community and the government has over time been transformed from a bottom-up control to a top-down influence.

The government's reformation of the polity in the eighties was to a large extent inspired by a technocratic concern for the management of resources and by the need for a pre-emptive defusion of the build-up of a racially based revolutionary coalition against the all-white State. This has been accompanied by the development of new constituencies in the brown, Indian and black communities, as well as in the corporate sector of the economy. The co-optation of some of the leadership elements from these sectors of society into the managerial systems of the State has locked the government into a new pattern of obligations and made it less sensitive to the parochial concerns and interests of Afrikanerdom. Accordingly, the solidarity underpinning it has shifted from a communal to a more utilitarian one. This has made the consensus supporting it more brittle and vulnerable but has made the keeper of the consensus, the State itself, stronger. (The response of the electorate to the Conservative Party bears testimony to this.)

Thus the State has become the major support base of the regime and the forces that are assembled under the auspices of the government are much wider in scope than the mediating institutions between the Afrikaner political community and the State. Its reformist animus is capitalist and technocratic, its social ontology built on the reification of race and ethnicity, its central concerns economic growth and political stability. It is with this regime model that it is soliciting support in the political market place, inside and outside the electoral arena.

Very few of the élite formations in the polity and none of those in the Afrikaner political community have defected from this model to the regime model offered by the major revolutionary contenders for political power. All of them are concerned with the deployment of alternatives which can *prevent* revolution, not *enhance* it. The Independents' emphasis is in support of the *gradual* liberalisation of the polity, the desegregation of society and the revitalising of the economy by reallocating resources away from sites where they are consumed by the clients of ethnic socialism, to sites where they can generate growth under capitalist management. The counter-revolutionary objective of this strategy is to deradicalise black élites by co-opting them into the capitalist economy, thereby reducing the salience of politics as a procedure to compete for material rewards. It offers a decentralised polity run on federal lines to protect middle-class political influence and economic privilege against the prospective demands of a central government responding to the pressures of a populist majority. It is pro-West and strives to lock itself firmly into the ostensibly benign embrace of the First World economies. Its supporters are disposed towards a careful and conservative strategy in seeking out political partners, and because it is a subordinate force in South African politics and unlikely to erect a regime on its own terms, it is far more likely to adopt the role of encouraging black support for a liberalised version of the present regime, than to facilitate a revolutionary alternative.

We offer tentative support for this perspective on the Independent phenomenon, on the basis of an empirical study conducted on the attitudes of students at the University of Stellenbosch a year before, and again a month after, the general election of 1987. The Stellenbosch constituency (with its contiguous neighbour Helderberg) formed the hub of the Independent onslaught on the National Party and it is here one is likely to observe its impact on electoral politics, its rationale, and the animus that constituted its driving force.

The nationwide decline of the National Party as the principal link between the Afrikaner political community and the political centre is evident from the support it has attracted from Stellenbosch students over the past 17 years.

Throughout the seventies the National Party could rely on the support of roughly 85 per cent of Afrikaner students; in 1981 it came down to 77 per cent, in 1986 to 73 per cent and in 1987 to just 67 per cent. Until the middle eighties the only party that made any inroads into this support was the PFP on the left. The PFP grew from a meagre 0,7 per cent in 1970 to a peak of 10 per cent support among Afrikaans students in 1981. However, after the referendum in 1983 it fell back to 7 per cent and with the advent of the Independent movement and the UDF on the far left of the spectrum, it lost further ground so that it now stands at 5 per cent. The UDF attracts some 3 per cent support among Afrikaner students and the Independent movement a further 15 per cent. This means that on our 1987 measurement almost 23 per cent of Afrikaans-speaking students found a political home to the left of the National Party. In 1970 this figure was 8 per cent, in 1974 (a bad election year for the National Party) it grew to 12 per cent, in 1981 it retained that level, in 1986 it had dropped further to about 8 per cent, until the initiative of the Independent movement and to a lesser extent the attractions of the UDF stimulated it to the proportions it assumed in 1987. Of all the students at Stellenbosch just on 30 per cent now identify with parties to the left of the National Party. Some 8 per cent lie to the right of the National Party, almost exclusively as supporters of the Conservative Party.

The pattern of support among English-speaking students during this same period shifted towards a greater acceptance of the National Party. The Party attracted a steady 18 per cent support from English-speaking students at Stellenbosch throughout the seventies and up to 1981. (It dipped to 8 per cent in 1974 when the NP had a temporary setback at the polls.) The 1983 referendum demonstrated major support among the English-speakers in South Africa for the government's initiatives to modernise the regime and by 1986 almost 40 per cent of English-speaking students at Stellenbosch considered themselves National Party supporters.

We interpret this as indicating the extent to which the English-speaking community has switched its allegiance to the regime model the government is deploying for the modernisation of the polity and the society, rather than as a defection to the National Party *per se*. The National Party has, since it assumed power in 1948, not just acted as the representative of the Afrikaner political community in the polity. Instead, it has gradually introduced a political regime based on its racist ideology, and in the process is not only attracting support in the political market place as a representative of the Afrikaner political community, but more so as the representative of this regime *and* the seat of power under this regime, namely the State itself. Under these conditions the major political choice in South Africa has become one between types of regimes, not political parties.

Using this as a context for interpretation we return to the role the Independent movement and its supporters can play under these conditions.

All the revolutionary challengers in South Africa offer majoritarian alternatives to the present system of government. One of the basic principles underlying the majority rule model is that it rejects a polity that makes provision for the constitutional protection of political, economic or cultural privileges on a group basis. An item in our 1987 Stellenbosch questionnaire that is compatible with this notion of the legitimate polity, gained 21 per cent support from the students. We called it the open democracy option.

The percentages for this and other options were as follows:

The establishment of a democratic system under which
all the peoples of South Africa will be allowed, *on an equal basis,*
to decide who shall govern the country.   21,3%

The total political integration of all the population groups
within the boundaries of a *federal State* which provides for the
protection of group rights.   34,9%

The creation of a system which establishes an overarching
structure of cooperation between South Africa and the
national States so that *self-determination* over *own affairs* for
the different population groups and *power-sharing* over
common affairs can be realised.   31,5%

Total political and geographical separation of the blacks,
coloureds, Indians and whites so that every group obtains
a territory that can develop into an *independent State.*   5,0%

Whites as the strongest group must continue to govern, with
only local control granted to other groups.   7,4%

Of the students who voted for Independent candidates in the 1987 elections,
37 per cent opted for what we termed the open democracy option, 51 per
cent preferred a group-based federal arrangement and close on 10 per cent
voted for the option reflecting official National Party policy. This puts the
majority in line with the options traditionally offered by the PFP and more
recently reflected in the Indaba proposals of Inkatha.

The African National Congress and the United Democratic Front are the
two major protagonists for a majoritarian democracy in South Africa and
the UDF has created opportunities for like-minded whites to join its ranks.
On an index that measures sympathy and antipathy towards these organisations (we used the so-called 'feeling thermometer'), 23 per cent of the Independent supporters reported sympathy with the ANC and 63 per cent
displayed hostility. For the UDF the figures were 30 per cent sympathy and
52 per cent antipathy. (This compares with 11 per cent sympathy and 83 per
cent hostility towards the ANC, and 14 per cent sympathy and 74 per cent
hostility towards the UDF in the total sample.)

At the same time the Zulu-based Inkatha movement has emerged as one
of the more vociferous opponents of the ANC and the UDF in the black communities of South Africa, both on the ideological and the political fronts.
Violent confrontations between UDF and Inkatha supporters are almost
daily occurrences in Natal. Similarly, the coloured Labour Party in the
House of Representatives and the two Indian parties in the House of Delegates (both State-sponsored institutions) are hostile to the UDF and regularly denounce this organisation in a style very similar to that of spokesmen
for the government.

Yet both Inkatha and the incumbents of the two Houses of Parliament are
very popular with the supporters of the Independent movement at Stellenbosch. Only 9 per cent of them feel any sense of hostility towards Inkatha
while some 76 per cent report sympathetic or very sympathetic feelings.
(The values in the total sample are 17 per cent hostility and 58 per cent sympathy towards Inkatha.) Similarly, around 60 per cent of them display sympathy for the coloured and Indian Houses and for the leaders in the so-called
homelands. Almost 60 per cent of the Independents also support the basic
guide-line by which these organisations have conducted their opposition
to the government: to work within the system and reform it from the inside.
(On these issues the Independents deviate only slightly from the values that
were recorded for the comprehensive student sample.)

The ANC and the UDF (not to mention other revolutionary organisations
like the PAC and Azapo) are both committed to the ideal of a socialist
economy for South Africa and have over the years displayed varying degrees of hostility to the role of large business corporations in providing

comfort to the South African regime. Only 7 per cent of the Independents share this hostility and 59 per cent are sympathetic towards the role of big business in the community. The others indicate indifference. (Values of 45 per cent sympathy and 10 per cent antipathy were recorded for big business corporations in the entire sample.)

The position people have adopted on the role of violence in the process of political change in South Africa has been a useful rule of thumb to decide their attitude towards a possible revolutionary transfer of political power. The ANC has declared violence an essential element of their overall strategy to put pressure on the State. The UDF, although publicly committed to peaceful political strategies, has yet to condemn the violence generated in the black communities against some of their political opponents and some of the authorities representing the State. The UDF has tended to excuse this violence as a legitimate form of retaliation against the sometimes violent methods of repression used by State agencies.

Only about 10 per cent of the Independents feel comfortable with this justification of political violence. Eighteen per cent agree with the proposition that terrorism and guerrilla action is frequently the only way by which a repressed group can get what they deserve, while only 8 per cent endorse the use of demonstrations and disruptions as methods to bring about necessary changes. Of the sample, 23 per cent accepted that the use of violence was probably the only way to bring about necessary change. When asked who was principally to blame for the violence in the black communities, 42 per cent blamed the government and 46 per cent blamed the ANC and the UDF. (In the total sample 17 per cent blamed the government and 72 per cent thought the ANC and the UDF were the villians.)

Among the Stellenbosch UDF supporters, 30 per cent endorse retaliatory violence, 58 per cent condone terrorism and guerilla action as legitimate tactics and 78 per cent accept the use of violence as a means to bring about change in South Africa. The government was blamed for the unrest in the townships by 85 per cent and the other 15 per cent ascribed township violence to the presence of the South African Defence Force (SADF) and the behaviour of the police.

The UDF has played an important role in the past few years to stimulate organised acts of public protest in the black communities. These included boycott action, public protest marches, rent strikes and industrial strike action. At the same time, the ANC has declared the disruption of the processes of government administration in the black townships and the mobilisation of the black communities into protest action against the State, as one of 'the four pillars' of their revolutionary strategy.

An index designed to measure what we termed repression potential (i.e. the extent to which respondents were prepared to justify the methods by which the State agencies repress acts of political protest and violence) revealed the following pattern:

	Total sample %	Independents %
Would endorse none of the measures undertaken by the State	19,9	37,9
Showed some repression potential	10,8	14,9
Showed high repression potential	45,0	34,5
Showed very high repression potential	24,2	12,7

(This index included items such as the breaking up of peaceful demonstrations by the police, the police shooting at demonstrators who damage property, deployment of the defence force to break strikes, eviction of people who refuse to pay rates, rents or taxes for political reasons, punishment by the courts of people who organised boycotts, and detaining people who participated in protest marches.)

On this evidence more than 60 per cent of the Independents supported one or other form of repressive action against the type of initiatives undertaken under the auspices of both the ANC and the UDF. This attitude contrasts sharply with the responses among the Stellenbosch supporters of the UDF where there was zero support for any of the repressive measures we mentioned. Among the supporters of the National Union of South African Students, Nusas (another organisation attractive to the white student left in South Africa), 95 per cent refused to endorse any of these measures. The Independents did, however, display a significantly lower repression potential than the average for the total sample, in which more than 80 per cent supported some or other form of repressive action.

Another important indicator of regime support is the attitude adopted towards the security establishment in the country, i.e. the defence force, the police and the security police. The order of the State and the identity of the political community that the SADF is duty bound to defend is based on the social ontology of Afrikaner nationalism. The enemies of this regime are typified as 'The Enemy'. Thus the ANC, an organisation with long-standing and deep roots in the black communities of South Africa and probably the one with the largest single political following in the country, is designated an enemy of 'South Africa' ... the South Africa of Afrikaner nationalism. The ANC and the UDF have also frequently and publicly denounced the political role of the SADF and sought to delegitimise it by discouraging military service and offering support to organisations like the End Conscription Campaign. Sympathy with the defence force can therefore be a useful indicator of regime loyalty. We calculated a Pearsons correlation coefficient of –,64 between the items measuring sympathy for the defence force and the ANC respectively.

Whereas 100 per cent of the UDF supporters at Stellenbosch and 67 per cent of Nusas members indicate hostile feelings towards the defence force, only 22 per cent of the Independents do so. Fifty-three per cent are sympathetic to the SADF and a further 25 per cent show indifference. (The distribution in the total sample is 76 per cent sympathetic, 13 per cent indifferent and 11 per cent antipathetic.)

For whites, accepting a majority rule model means accepting that black political élites will in future wield significant and probably decisive political power in the polity. To tap feelings towards this prospect, we used an index comprising 25 items which required respondents to evaluate the conditions and quality of life they expected to experience under a white-controlled and a black-controlled government respectively. On this index 60 per cent of the total Stellenbosch sample gave a white-controlled government a high to very high score, 19 per cent were neutral and 21 per cent gave it a low to very low score. A prospective black-controlled government was given a low to very low score by 66 per cent of the students with 21 per cent neutral and 12 per cent in the high to very high categories.

The pattern for the Independent movement, National Party and UDF supporters appeared as follows:

White-controlled government

	NP	Ind.	UDF	Total sample
	%	%	%	%
High score	78,7	29	0	60
Neutral	15,1	29,1	3,5	18,8
Low score	6,2	41,9	96,5	21,5
	n = 466	n = 146	n = 29	n = 801

Black-controlled government

	NP	Ind.	UDF	Total sample
	%	%	%	%
High score	5,6	20	86,3	12,4
Neutral	17,8	30,5	3,7	21,2
Low score	76,6	49,5	0	66,4
	n = 466	n = 146	n = 29	n = 801

Ind. = Independents

Unlike the supporters of the UDF and the National Party, the Independents do not exhibit a clear bias towards either white or black control of the polity.

A group of about 63 to 65 per cent record feelings of neutrality or dissatisfaction with a state of affairs where either whites or blacks control the government.

This disposition can further be illustrated by a breakdown of the average scores the supporters of the different political parties gave black-controlled and white-controlled governments respectively. On a scale of 1 to 7 for each of these two indices, the following results were obtained:

Average score for a black-controlled government by party preference

NP	HNP	NRP	CP	PFP	Ind.	UDF
2,0	1,0	1,9	1,5	2,9	2,6	4,7

Average score for a white-controlled government by party preference

4,2	5,1	4,7	4,8	2,4	2,8	1,5

Average difference (+) denotes white, and (–) denotes black preference

NP	HNP	NRP	CP	PFP	Ind.	UDF
+2,2	+4,1	+2,8	+3,3	–0,5	+0,2	–3,2

By using factor analysis techniques we were able to establish that all the major variables in our study that in some or other way tapped attitudes which were associated with trust in government, the legitimacy of the system of government, the behaviour of the South African government and its major opponents, racial attitudes and policy preferences could be explained by one single factor: regime loyalty and support. This factor was a composite of attitudes towards political protest, state coercion, the legitimacy of extra-parliamentary opposition to the regime, sympathy towards the major institutions of government, trust in government, policy preference, a left–right continuum of political attitudes, a left–right continuum based on party identification, attitudes towards the security establishment, and the attitudes towards black- and white-controlled governments referred to above. In the grand old tradition of South African political analysis we called this summary variable 'The Laager'. Our respondents were classified into one of five categories: deep inside, comfortably inside, agonising inside, agonising outside and well outside. The total distribution was as follows:

Deep inside	18,8%
Comfortably inside	50,4%
Agonising inside	19,2%
Agonising outside	8,2%
Well outside	3,3%

The distribution for the major political party groupings looked like this:

	NP	CP	NRP	PFP	Ind.	UDF
	%	%	%	%	%	%
Deep inside (1)	25,1	31,9	29,2	0	0	0

	NP	CP	NRP	PFP	Ind.	UDF
Comfortable inside (2)	64,4	64,5	41,7	9,1	30,3	0
Agonising inside (3)	10	3,6	29,2	39,8	48	0
Agonising outside (4)	0,5	0	0	45,3	18,9	30
Well outside (5)	0	0	0	5,8	2,9	70

A breakdown of the average score of the various parties (between 1 and 5 from 'inside' to 'outside') shows the Herstigte Nasionale Party at 1,0, the Conservative Party at 1,7, the National Party at 1,8, the NRP at 2,0, the Independents at 2,9, the PFP at 3,4 and the UDF at 4,7. This can give one a grasp of where the supporters of the Independent movement at Stellenbosch University would be placed within the wider pattern of support for the Botha regime. They may be defectors from the National Party but they remain fundamentally committed to the regime.[2]

NOTES

[1] *Sechaba*, October 1987.

[2] The surveys on which these results are based were conducted by the author using representative sampling methods. The most recent study conducted in 1987 was based on a sample of 801 students. Responses were obtained using a self-completion questionnaire. The response rate was 70 per cent.

7

THE EXTRA-PARLIAMENTARY MOVEMENT: STRATEGIES AND PROSPECTS

Mark Swilling

In this chapter I shall review the strategies and prospects of the extra-parliamentary movement in terms of the theme of conflict resolution through negotiations. My argument will be based on a systematic critique of a single commonly held proposition in South African politics:

To compel one's opponent to negotiate, he must be weakened to the point where he has no alternative but to capitulate.

The above is often held alongside two other strategic propositions, namely, (i) negotiations equal capitulation, and (ii) negotiations should only be used to divide and hence weaken the opponent. I will only be addressing the first proposition because in many ways the case for the other two is substantially weakened when the first falls away.

My aim will be to make a case for the contrary position, namely that free association and the right to organise is a necessary precondition for negotiations.

There are basically three fundamental pillars of the extra-parliamentary movement: the trade unions with their base in the factories, the UDF with its base in the communities and the ANC which is rooted in an impressive international diplomatic network but also has a substantial underground structure within the country.

The contemporary trade union movement has its roots in the Durban strikes of 1973. From then until 1979 the black trade union movement grew, was strengthened and developed largely outside a formal collective bargaining machinery. The basic strategy was the principle that unionists should stick to organising around workplace issues in order to win a base in the factories. Once that had been achieved, pressure could be brought to bear on the State to amend the labour relations legislation so that black trade unions could be fully recognised.

This strategy worked for one simple reason: labour, capital and the State found themselves in a power relationship where compromise through negotiations was the only option. How did this come about? To summarise a familiar story: over a period of years and despite State and managerial resistance, unionists painstakingly established an organisational base in the factories. Management then realised that negotiating with trade unions was preferable to smashing them. The State accepted the Wiehahn analysis that the old system of in-house liaison and works committees was not working and that a collective bargaining system, premised on the necessity for negotiations between organised labour and capital, was desirable. The result: a successful system where groups with opposing interests resolve conflict on the basis that each has the right to organise, protest, make demands and then negotiate and compromise.

The UDF grew out of a completely different dynamic, the result of the intersection of two critically important social tensions. The first related to the impact of the new constitution on black political consciousness. The exclusion of the African majority coupled with the steady delegitimation of the homelands, left the black majority without a channel through which to express political grievances. The UDF emerged to provide this channel and in so doing drew black political consciousness into a world-view dominated by ideologies, symbols and leaders whose roots lay in a long tradition of resistance stretching back to the founding of the ANC in 1912. Even the government now accepts that the tricameral parliament is not the final solution.

The second social tension was essentially socio-economic in nature. With the acceptance of the Riekert framework that was premised on the acceptance of the permanence of the urban black insiders, a range of reforms were conceded. These included rights to permanent residence, intra-urban labour mobility, improved trading facilities, trade union association, property and most importantly, the franchise at local level via the black local authorities (BLAs). However, these reforms began to be implemented as the economy was slipping out of the 1979–82 boom and tumbling into a recession. By 1983 the State did not have the funds to finance reform at township level and so coupled the right to self-determination at local level with the principle of financial self-sufficiency. We all know what happened then: when councillors tried to increase rents and service charges to raise money, the nationwide rebellion of 1984 to 1986 was triggered. As early as 1985 a senior government official conceded that it 'was a mistake not to give the BLAs resources of magnitude'.

The rebellion of 1984–86 was fuelled by this potent combination of political and socio-economic grievances. The UDF emerged as the national ideological and political centre of this social movement. To this extent it has played a crucial role because the social movement that made the UDF what it is, has blown the fuses of white complacency and short-circuited the constitutional, urban and economic reforms that were an expression of the Total Strategy in the early 1980s.

Common perceptions of the township rebellions amongst whites are of mob violence, irrational boycott-tactics, fiery incomprehensible leaders and communist agitators. Very few understand the logic of township protest and where it is leading to. I participated in a detailed study of 30 instances of township conflict. It was an Urban Foundation project that took more than 18 months to complete. I found, contrary to what the agitator thesis holds, that township conflict went through the following stages ultimately leading, in many cases, to negotiations.

- Grievances were expressed about appalling living conditions in the community. When these were not addressed by councillors, eminent persons would present the grievances to local officials in the form of a petition or simply a verbal articulation of problems. It is important to note that at this stage collective organisation had not yet taken place.
- The authorities either ignored or rebuked the petitioners, frequently on spurious grounds such as bureaucratic procedure. The most destructive response was when officials made promises that were never kept.
- In reaction to the local authority's inadequate response, leadership groups emerged to organise the different layers of the community. This resulted in the formation and expansion of civic organisations, youth congresses, women's groups and other similar structures.
- Campaigns involving collective action took place, e.g. mass meetings, demonstrations, stayaways, and consumer boycotts. Essentially what happened was that after the failure to affect public opinion through the Press, in Parliament, through access to intellectual/research structures or through other channels, the poor communities responded by mobilising their only resource, namely their collective capacity to disturb, disrupt and protest.
- Collective action in the communities was met with repression as the security forces moved in. When the security personnel overreacted and used excessive violence, the counter-response was even more destructive.
- A spiral of violence erupted as the rather dignified protests of previous phases gave way to running street battles between militant youths and the security forces. When this was accompanied by the detention of the civic leaders, the youth became completely uncontrollable and the spiral of violence was exacerbated.
- Decentralised defence structures were established in the community which soon transformed themselves into what later became known as the street and area committees. By this stage, the rupture between State and community was virtually complete.
- A stalemate set in as repressive action failed to break the resistance, and as the communities failed to find ways of getting the authorities to recognise their demands.

In most cases the conflict levelled off at this point of stalemate. However, in many of the cases, groupings in the local white and black establishments made tentative moves to resolve the stalemate through negotiations. The most successful local-level negotiations were those that took place where authorities had resigned themselves to the existence of mass organisation in the townships and where the local black leadership felt they had the support and a mandate from their constituencies to talk to local white leaders. This happened in places such as Port Elizabeth, Port Alfred, Uitenhage, East London, Oudtshoorn, Worcester, Kirkwood and Cradock. The negotiations took place between local UDF leaders and white leaders ranging from local chambers of commerce, local township administrators, white municipal representatives, right up to NP MPs, the deputy director-general of Constitutional Development and Planning, and Minister Heunis himself.

The basic point is simple: as in the trade union context, negotiations took place only after both sides had realised that negotiation was less costly and more stable than the continuation of a stalemate situation. The negotiations did not follow directly after the wholesale repression of the township organisations, nor had the local power structures in the white community been substantially weakened.

I would like to draw from the conclusions of an as yet unpublished study undertaken by myself and colleagues on the topic of community negotiations. Once community organisations have, in effect, taken 'political and ideological' control of the township, they do not have coercive control. They therefore have a choice: they can take on the State and risk a total confrontation, or reach temporary accommodation with the State. The former option would involve turning the townships into liberated zones. However, in the absence of a permanent 'people's army' to defend these zones in ways seen in northern Mozambique during the anti-colonial war, the communities had no chance of winning a confrontation. The result would have been the immediate repression of their organisations.

The alternative, therefore, lay in demanding recognition as the representatives of the community. This is a classic pattern of power distribution during times of intense conflict and struggle. Examples in world history are of the Paris Commune in 1848, the Soviets in Russia in 1917, Barcelona's communes during the Spanish Civil War, and the US ghetto revolts of the 1960s (which is where the term 'ungovernability' was first used). Lenin referred to such a situation as one of 'dual power' because, as happened between the Provisional government and the Soviets before October 1917, the existing duly constituted State agrees to recognise a rival power. This arrangement is usually transitional and will only culminate in a revolution if the security forces cease backing the State (as in Russia). However, in cases where the security forces remain loyal but are not used to smash the alternative power structure, 'dual power' can lead to negotiation and greater democratisation as the opposition powers are absorbed on terms more favourable than when they rejected the status quo in the first place. This is what happened as regards the US ghettos, the South American squatter movements, the Spanish Citizens Movement during the 1970s, the Philippino protest movements after Marcos, Solidarity in Poland, Mau Mau in Kenya, the guerrillas in Zimbabwe and many others.

The implications of this process in the South African context are far-reaching to say the least. It boils down to the fact that movements can only be revolutionary when they operate under revolutionary conditions. Although the social movements were smashed despite their desire to negotiate, a less repressive and a more democratic long-term alternative was available.

In the light of the above, the following conclusions can be drawn:

- The State completely misread what was happening in the townships. Relying on the distorted information being fed from right-wing security policemen on the ground, and seduced by the militance of township rhetoric, the State mistook township protest for revolution and reacted accordingly but, tragically, completely inappropriately.

- The state of emergency will only increase the level of endemic violence. As with previous clampdowns, the result is always greater violence: Umkhonto We Sizwe was established after the banning of the ANC in 1960; the ANC was invigorated after the 1977 clampdown on the black consciousness movement that sent thousands into exile, resulting in two-thirds of present ANC membership in exile being of the post-1976 generation; and now, in 1987, we await the consequences of the 1986 clampdown. My prediction is that, given that nearly all the real leaders who could control the situation are in detention, this violence will develop internally, will not be organised by established groups, nor will it be undertaken by disciplined ANC cadres constrained by the distinction between hard and soft targets. In short, repression breeds radicalism, not the desire to negotiate.

- As far as the extra-parliamentary movement as a whole is concerned, it is weaker and less organised than before on the ground, but its internal organisations remain committed to non-violence. These continue to command widespread support and although lacking in organisational infrastructure because of repression, I have no doubt they will prevent the National Council from succeeding in its mission.

  Externally the ANC will continue the armed struggle but will take advantage of its international position to increase pressure on the government to accept the need for a negotiated settlement. This can only succeed if the movements in the townships manage to survive the current clampdown. If not, then I agree with the conclusion Stephen Davis arrives at in his new book (1987), that the younger, more radical generation may well gain the upper hand in the ANC and then seek to turn the movement away from its current policy of moderation.

In short, the initiative lies with the government. By clamping down on what it thought was a revolution, it missed a critical moment for negotiations because, as I have tried to demonstrate here, negotiations do not take place when the opponent has been weakened, but rather when he is confident that he can talk with the support of an organised base. For those who want to take the High Road seriously, it must be accepted that the current clampdown on township resistance is the single biggest obstacle they will need to clear out of the way. At this moment the damage is not irreversible, but it soon will be.

REFERENCE

Davis S, *Apartheid rebels: inside South Africa's hidden war*, New Haven, Yale University Press, 1987.

8

THE YOUTH IN THE EXTRA-PARLIAMENTARY OPPOSITION

Paulus Zulu

INTRODUCTION

In South Africa the extra-parliamentary opposition has a unique and distinctive role; unique in that it exists at all, because the parliamentary decision-making system is not open; distinctive in that it is seeking a transformation of rather than inclusion into the established socio-political and economic systems. Black people, in particular, challenge the neutrality of the State as an arbiter in conflicts centred around group interests, since differential incorporation into the decision-making process is predicated upon race where whites have monopoly of power over all the other races in the country. In essence therefore, blacks in South Africa can be regarded as non-citizens. This chapter looks into the role of the black youth as central actors within the popular section of the extra-parliamentary opposition movement.* It examines both the socio-political and socio-economic origins of the youth in protest, as well as the strategic logic underpinning their quest for an alternative to their present voicelessness.

During the past ten years in South Africa, the conception that the task of shaping and directing the affairs of society is the prerogative of the country's mature citizens has been overturned gradually. The black youth have entered the socio-political arena as a major and active force. Instead of assuming their traditional subsidiary role, they are shaping township politics: they have taken the political initiative from the older generation. Since 1976 this has had a major impact at every level of South African politics.

Other countries, too, have had their 'student revolts'. But while there may be superficial similarities there are many important differences as well. For example, the American and European student revolts in the sixties occurred at the universities while the terrain of political struggle in South Africa has been the schools. In its causes as well as in its implications, the black youth's revolt is a unique and typically South African phenomenon, and its characteristics can be traced to the nature of South African society itself.

---

* The analysis has been informed by ongoing research conducted by the author, and by various works which are listed in the references.

The present phase of the youth's struggle against apartheid – in which we have been involved since 1976 – has its philosophical roots in the ideology of black consciousness (BC). From the universities where it developed, it swiftly spread to the schools. This was no wonder. Given BC's own origins in the educational structure itself – and the central role that very system played in the perpetuation of apartheid – mobilising students around educational issues was both necessary and possible.

Together with the spread of black consciousness, economic conditions were also making the youth increasingly restive. The economic boom of the late sixties to the early seventies led to a greater need for skilled workers. This necessitated increased investment not only in white, but especially in black education. Ironically, the increase in numbers in African schools further revealed the contradictions in a racist society. By the time the recession of the late seventies was setting in, large numbers of black youths were receiving secondary education – and hence were more politicised than before. It is from this newly politically conscious and militant youth that the present wave of unrest springs.

But this still does not fully explain the extent to which the youth are mobilised. What lies behind their determination to take on the South African government? It is true, of course, that the youth are a particularly idealistic segment of society, and that they are a group relatively unburdened with social responsibilities. It is also true that their natural sense of adventure – their willingness to take risks – plays a role. It is fun, it is adventure, to go out into the streets – and that thrill is intensified when they go in quest of an ideal. But to attribute their actions only to idealism is to ignore the political realities of the country. The adventurousness and idealism run parallel and in opposition to something else: an existential despair, their knowledge that as long as the present system exists, they have no future.

The black youth's idealism is, therefore, born of political knowledge. They are aware of their environment, they see that their white counterparts, upon leaving school, have some sort of a future: they have somewhere to go, something to look forward to. But the black youths have nowhere to go. Those from the rural areas are forced to go to the city in search of employment, which is frequently not available. The urban youths know that when they leave school, they enter a world in which there are no employment opportunities. They, too, become part of that lumpenproletariat, roaming the streets. They are landless and rightless, because they are black. It is a despair unknown to whites.

It is true that there are important social divisions among the young black people. They are not a monolithic entity that always act together. Not all of them take to the streets: some have petty bourgeois aspirations, and go or try to go to university. But there is one overriding factor that unites them: they will all take to the streets when the time is ripe. They are all blacks in an apartheid society that denies them their very humanity.

This is why they continually insist that they are human beings first of all: not Pedis, or Xhosas, or even blacks. They see themselves as black only to the extent that they are defined as black in the South African system, which does not mean that they see their blackness as a curse. They see it, on the contrary, as a challenge, something to be given a positive definition. And this means fighting for their rights as members of the human race.

The black youth are committed to non-racialism in a very real and basic sense. Even the policemen, both white and black, they encounter in the townships are seen as the enemy, mainly because of the system they represent. Correspondingly, those opposed to the present system are seen as allies, regardless of race. Coupled with this non-racialism there is a strong egalitarian trend in their thought. Born into oppression they are determined to transform South Africa into a society of equals.

There are two points one could make about their form of non-racialism. Firstly, it is not merely a rejection of racism, as a political strategy, it may also be regarded as an expression of confidence. In a transformed South Africa, black people will not have much to fear from other groups, for the simple reason that they will be the majority, and there will be no need for securing group rights. They can afford to stand for a non-racial society, which is of course what the world wants to hear.

The second point is that the youth's attitude to whites flows from a sense of realism about group relations at this time. Though it is confidently assumed that blacks will be the ruling majority in a future South Africa, their current position is one of material weakness. In such a position it does not make good tactical sense to alienate potential allies. The black youth recognise that they are going to need the whites and their skills, now and in the new South Africa. And the black youth realise that even should a time come when whites no longer monopolise essential skills, they will still be around. Contrary to what the government would like us to believe, the youth do not wish to drive the whites into the sea. All the imperatives point towards taking a conciliatory course.

The youth tend to see themselves as part of an indivisible mass movement. Whatever divisions might exist in their ranks are played down. This could be seen as a result of the imperatives of the mobilising game, but it is also due to the nature of oppression in South Africa. Even when we prepare the black youth for university we are not preparing them for managerial positions. They are – although at different levels – all workers. And under the present dispensation they will always be workers, they will always be living in the townships. Even those who escape the townships are bound to the working class with hoops of steel. Some might have escaped, but their relatives have not. Hence the term 'the people' refers not only to the working masses and the unemployed, but also to those blacks that have made it despite the present system. They refuse to recognise any division between social élites and the masses.

It is important to realise how central politics is to this self-definition, to what extent all terms are politically loaded. Usually, when one talks about what it means to be human, one is not concerned with politics. But when the youth define themselves being, in the first place, human, they are in fact making a political statement, because political oppression pervades the whole social system and their whole life. Votelessness means life in the township in a four-roomed house where the only playing-fields are the streets. To define oneself as human is self-definition in terms of the rights one is denied. Nothing is apolitical because apartheid is all-pervasive.

The youth's rejection of capitalism is also in part influenced by this reaction against their world. Apartheid society happens to be capitalist, so they opt for socialism. Admittedly, their political views on this point are partly influenced by intellectuals – but it is, to a large degree, simply an existential rejection of the present system.

The nature of the youth's commitment to socialism does not preclude their acceptance of, say, a mixed economy in the South Africa of the future. But this might change: they might be radicalised to the point where they are fully committed to a socialist system for South Africa. But at the moment they are not socialist ideologues, they are existential socialists. Everything is still conditioned by their existential reaction to their surroundings.

The same is true of their vision of the future. There is no clear political programme, no idea of how change will be implemented. The present reality is so hopeless that the only future worth struggling for is one which is, in all respects, the opposite of the present system. There is very little thought about the nuts and bolts of the future system. It is a millennial vision, something like the Promised Land or the Kingdom of God.

This is true of the adults as well. Even the most politically inarticulate of them express the hope that conditions would be better for their children than they were for them, the parents.

If the black youth are vague about the details of the future of South Africa, they are also vague as to how it shall come about. One is struck by the euphoria, the confidence, in their talk, as if the government were on the verge of collapse, as if liberation were around the corner. However, they are not coming much closer to their ideal. They are chipping away at the rock, but talk as if they were about to smash the whole edifice. Any shifts and concessions by the government – no matter how minute – are regarded as yet another stride forward on the road to victory.

In part, this phenomenon, too, is attributable to the imperatives of mobilisation. In their position, the youth need to be armed with a whole arsenal of moral victories. A march to the inspector's office without being stopped by the police and the ability to put demands clearly is seen as a moral victory. A much clearer victory would be if the police tried to stop the march and a confrontation ensued. Being the losers in this confrontation does not constitute any moral loss. The mere fact that they wanted to prevent the march shows how strong the case is, and how scared they are. The state of emergency, far from being a major blow to the struggle, is taken as a sign of the significance of the black youth.

The other reason is that such optimism is the only alternative to despair. This is why the present mood of the black youth poses such a problem to the government. People in such a hopeless position and subjected to such continuous oppression, cannot be stopped from rising up against the system. Thus far, several states of emergency could not stop them. It is like trying to dam up a river: it can only be contained for a while; sooner or later it will find its way through to the sea. There is always a way for a determined people to overcome obstacles in their way.

Of course, the black youth also sustain casualties. Being involved in such violent and bitter conflict is a brutalising experience. Fatima Meer, writing about the Iranian revolution, says that while the pride of every mother in South Africa is to see her son graduate from university, the pride of every mother in Iran is to see her son turned into a martyr. Something like that is happening here. A certain kind of stoicism is becoming more and more common. At political funerals there is very little weeping, but much shouting of slogans and speech-making. Death has acquired a political meaning; it is simply seen as part of a larger process. People simply accept that in a struggle of this kind there will be casualties.

Attitudes to violence have also changed. It is no longer seen as something that should only be used as a last resort. This is hardly surprising: violence is part of the structure of our society; it has been institutionalised. The State employs violent means; violence is perpetrated at the schools.

But this is not to say that the youth involved in the struggle are killers; in fact, many of them are not very violent at all, and their plans for, say, a street march, almost never include violence. By and large they plan demonstrations and defiance, and in many instances violence only erupts when the police confront them. Whether this will remain so for much longer is doubtful, as there has already been an increase in sophisticated forms of violence, with ever younger people being the culprits.

The only thing that might stop this tendency is a total transformation of the structures of this society. The present reforms are not going to help because, by definition, reform is unilateral. Reform always happens on the terms dictated by those in power, who see to it that they remain in power. It might be a dialectical process in the sense that the government is forced to reform its structures. But it is never a process by which significant power is ceded to the oppressed, and until that happens, the youth will continue to play the role they do now.

Concessions such as freehold rights in Soweto do not significantly change the plight of the black oppressed. People still have to return to their houses in the townships, they still have to travel long distances to work, and still face a hopeless future.

The greater the crisis within the culture and the more the State responds with repression, the greater will be the youth's resolve to continue with the struggle, until a peaceful, just and democratic South Africa is created.

REFERENCES

Gaventa J, *Power and powerlessness: Quiescence and rebellion in an Appalachian valley*, Oxford: Clarendon Press, 1980.

Hughes H, and Grest J, 'The Local State' in *South African Review One*, Johannesburg: Ravan Press, 1983.

Kuper L, *An African bourgeoisie: Race, class and politics in South Africa*, Yale University Press, 1965.

South African Institute of Race Relations Survey, 1983.

South African Institute of Race Relations Survey, 1985.

Zulu P M, 'Political Conflict and Unrest in African Townships: The Case of Natal', Maurice Webb Race Relations Unit. University of Natal. Durban (unpublished), 1987.

Zulu P M, 'International Resistance Movements. South Africa Beyond Apartheid', paper prepared for the project 'South Africa Beyond Apartheid' (unpublished), Centre for Applied Social Science, University of Natal, Durban, 1987.

Zulu P M, Ngidi S, and Booth D G, 'Political Resistance and Unrest in African Townships: Natal and the Eastern Cape', paper prepared for 'South Africa beyond Apartheid' (unpublished), 1987.

9

REFORM AND REVOLT: 1983 TO 1988

F van Zyl Slabbert

In this chapter the issue of resistance and revolt, and its interaction with the government's reform programme will be considered. Reference will be made to two phases, the first starting in 1983/4 with the introduction of the constitution and extending up to the imposition of the second State of Emergency in mid-1986. The second one started in June 1986 but acquired a clear definition only by the beginning of 1988. By this time the government had succeeded in restoring a large measure of 'order' and felt strong enough to impose wide-ranging political restrictions on the UDF and 17 other organisations.

1. THE PERIOD 1983/4 TO 1986

In considering the interaction between reform and revolt, it is appropriate to begin with the UDF, not because it is the oldest opposition movement (it is not) or necessarily the first to respond to the State's reform proposals, but because the UDF managed to capture the high ground in mobilising domestic resistance to the implementation of the new tricameral constitution. In doing so, it highlighted the fundamental cleavages between parliamentary and extra-parliamentary politics and posed a crisis of legitimacy for all individuals or organisations participating in State-created constitutional structures. The issue of black exclusion from the new tricameral constitution was effectively seized upon to question the relevance of any participation in such structures and to highlight the co-optative nature of the State's constitutional programme.

The diversity of organisations belonging to the UDF, as well as the rapidity with which its membership increased, made it difficult to judge in terms of a single policy or agenda. Gradually, however, 'critical issues' emerged which became identified with the UDF: The Freedom Charter, a pro-sanctions stand, non-racialism and a very sympathetic stance towards the ANC, although the UDF insisted that it was not an ANC front and was committed to non-violent opposition. Nevertheless, it campaigned vigorously for the unbanning of political organisations such as the ANC, and for the release of political prisoners. There is no doubt that the effective mass mobilisation by the UDF achieved two things which also characterised the nature of the revolt that accompanied reform, i.e. firstly, it defined the revolt as a struggle between an extra-parliamentary executive (i.e. State President plus State Security Council plus security forces) and extra-parliamentary opposition groups, and secondly, it forced the South African State to propagandize the ANC as the 'vanguard of the total onslaught'.

From 16 to 23 June 1985 there was a Second National Consultative Conference of the ANC in Lusaka. From its proceedings as documented in Committee Reports, a comprehensive picture of the ANC structures, code of conduct, strategies and tactics as well as membership emerges.

Given the encompassing nature of the ANC strategies, it is inevitable that it will become involved in any significant internal resistance and revolt, and that ANC supporters/members will be active either openly or clandestinely across a wide spectrum of movements, fronts, organisations and activities. That is why strikes, consumer and school boycotts, protest meetings, etc., initiated by other organisations, but with the same issues at stake, will enjoy ANC support and even active participation. In this sense, it sometimes becomes irrelevant whether the UDF is an ANC front or not. A spokesman for the ANC made this quite clear: 'What the UDF has been doing is part of this growing resistance to the apartheid system, the struggle to bring about a new order. We are happy with that ... I think the UDF represents the success of our appeals to our people to be organised and to unite in action. That doesn't make them ANC, but they have got to fight the struggle.'

The same applies to any other single-purpose organisation pursuing a line of action that falls within the ANC's broad definition of the struggle, whether it be the Black Sash, the End Conscription Campaign, a trade union, a church or even the PFP. This is an important point because by choosing the ANC as its prime opponent, the South African State by implication demonises or denounces as criminals any opposition group or strategy the actions of which correspond with goals or strategies of the ANC. In fact, given the goals and strategies of the South African State and the ANC respectively, it is quite evident that each defines the other as the prime target of its total strategy. The 'total strategy' of the State is the National Security Management System (NSMS) and the reform programme. The 'total strategy' of the ANC is the National Democratic Revolution for a liberated South Africa. The final objective of each strategy is the destruction of the other. That is why reform and revolt will continue to interact with each other until this cycle is somehow broken.

An important consequence of the State targeting the ANC as its major opponent is that it can propagandize against any other party or organisation which shares values in common with ANC objectives. Thus the issues of 'one man one vote', non-racial democracy, freedom of association, unbanning of organisations, the rule of law and the civil liberties of the individual as opposed to the 'rights of the group' immediately make a party or organisation which campaigns for them suspect, either as being 'useful idiots' or willing collaborators of the ANC. At the same time, the State can select aspects of ANC strategy or structure for demonising purposes, and through guilt by association tar any other opposition grouping with the same brush. 'Terrorism', 'violence' and 'communism' are the three most common labels.

It is particularly in the white political arena where this rather crude tactic is very effective. A 1985 survey of the Human Sciences Research Council (HSRC) amongst white voters indicated that 85 per cent were in favour of 'negotiating with blacks'. However, only 4 per cent of respondents believed that it should be with the ANC. White voters are not only conditioned to think that negotiation *need not* include the ANC, but are constantly brainwashed to believe that any negotiation with the ANC should be avoided at all costs. The ANC is officially presented in South Africa as a gang of incorrigible villains that must be eliminated and with whom the State should not negotiate at any cost.

This approach by the State more than anything else lies at the root of its inability to attract credible leaders into any of its co-optative structures, such as the tricameral parliament and National Council. Any party or organisation that petitions for the unbanning of the ANC and negotiating with it, is condemned as wanting to hob-nob with 'terrorists' and 'communists'. The violent means employed by the government are based on the theory that the total onslaught against the State needs to be countered by a total strategy, which includes a policy of co-optation, control and patronage. The State has a crisis of legitimacy and would like to reform away from this, although it is not too concerned about it as long as its control is not threatened.

The ANC gives articulate, historical reasons for their strategy of violence. Their means consist of forms of unconventional war and strike action. They have a degree of strategic inflexibility because should they abandon the armed struggle, sanctions, etc., they would have support problems. The ANC policy is therefore bound by its organisational structures. The political conflict in South Africa can be depicted in the following terms:

REFORM	REVOLT
1. Creates a *group-based* democracy.	1. Creates an *individual-based* democracy.
2. Concerned with reform *within* State structures.	2. Concerned with reform *of* State structures.
3. Broadens participation through *co-optation.*	3. Broadens participation through *negotiation.*
4. Wants to *multi-racialise* South Africa.	4. Wants to *de-racialise* South Africa.
5. *Adjusts* white domination.	5. *Removes* white domination.

The ultimate objective of reform is to establish a multi-racial government of an *autocratic* nature; the ultimate objective of revolt is to establish a non-racial government of a *democratic* nature. Those caught up in revolt may differ amongst themselves about the nature of that democracy and the socio-economic structure of society which is to accompany it, but there is unanimity of purpose that the alternative should be democratic and non-racial. Those concerned with reform and the 'total strategy' may differ amongst themselves about the scope and quality of reform, but have unanimity of purpose that white minority control must not be sacrificed under any circumstances. (See diagram opposite.)

2. THE PERIOD 1986 TO 1988

This period began with the declaration of the second State of Emergency which paved the way for massive State repression. By the beginning of 1988 the State had managed to quell most of the open revolt. In February 1988 it proscribed the political activities of a whole range of extra-parliamentary organisations. It also tabled legislation aimed at cutting off foreign funding of a variety of organisations.

This means that the State is not going to allow itself to be challenged directly or at the centre – it has made that quite clear. Any central-focus challenge will be dealt with ruthlessly. We have come to the end of an era as far as resistance or opposition politics is concerned – the end of protest or mass mobilisation politics which directly challenges the authorities. Through these restrictions, the government crushed those popularly-based organisations that symbolically challenged the role of the State or that could be used to mobilise people to do so. They have also made it increasingly difficult, if not impossible, for similar kinds of organisations to obtain funding from overseas.

What the State is trying to do, therefore, is to portray and treat as criminal all dissent that does not arise within the structures it condones or is prepared to create. Thereafter it tries to deal with opposing parties inside those structures.

It would be very short-sighted to see these actions as similar to those taken against organisations in 1960 or 1977. The main difference is that some of the major liberal, supporting institutions that resisted the State are no longer there, or have changed substantially.

The courts have been fundamentally affected over the past 27 years. People no longer have the same access, since all the amending legislation on security removed much of the jurisdiction from the courts. Parliament is not half as accountable as it used to be, because a mass of enabling legislation has removed whole areas of control from Parliament, with the result that the government just cannot be questioned, e.g. on funds, activities, and matters that are 'not in the national interest'.

REFORM AND REVOLT

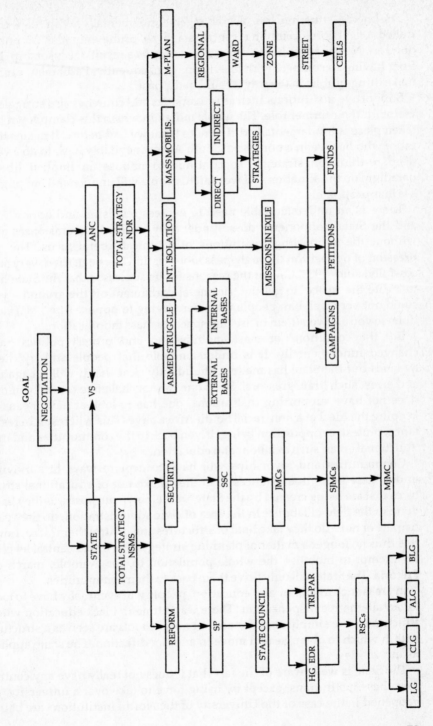

The media situation has also changed fundamentally, with state-controlled television occupying centre stage as prime moulder of public opinion. Newspapers have suffered, not only as a result of censorship, but from having to compete with television. Consequently, Parliament cannot make things public in the way it could in the past.

Supportive institutions such as universities and churches also struggle to maintain their former role. The whole milieu in which this clampdown has taken place is fundamentally different to what we had before. It means that those who believe in a non-racial South Africa inevitably have to do a very deep re-think on strategy. To continue to impose an implicit liberal paradigm on the situation – 'If we march, people will understand our plight' – is inappropriate.

There is an understandable need to express revulsion and opposition, and the State's opponents do so under very unequal circumstances and without the supporting institutions of a typical liberal focus. The expression of opposition through mass mobilisation has been tried, very successfully, since 1983. One of the reasons for its success is that the State had to create the 'space' to get the tricameral parliament off the ground – you could not very well ban people who were trying to oppose (the 1984) elections so you allowed them to use that space for mass mobilisation.

But the conditions of mass mobilisation and protest politics have changed fundamentally. It is understandable that people still try these avenues but the State has made it abundantly clear that it will act against and arrest such 'transgressors'. So, if one cannot challenge centrally, if one does not have supporting institutions, one has to look at new means of keeping the ideal of a non-racial South Africa alive. This will result in resistance, protest, or opposition being driven back to the communities and into 'functional areas' such as labour and education.

Communities and townships will have to explore ways of surviving under these new circumstances. Can they make use of educational structures that are being created by the State for their own purposes, as they have done in the field of labour? In the area of civic administration, do they participate or not – do they take hold of structures and control them? If so, how? It is thus no longer a matter of planning strategy on a broad central level in an attempt to mobilise the whole population to, for example, march on Pretoria. The State will only drive them back to their communities.

In areas such as labour and education, people will eventually have to look for an alternative dispensation. There was a time in black education when structures were simply abandoned, but now schools are seen as a structure within which to organise and move in another direction. The same applies to universities.

The State is well aware of the fact that it does not really have any control over these institutions, except by using force to take over a university, as happened in the case of the University of the North. Institutions are being shaped and mauled in the struggle and a suitable response will have to be sought.

Inevitably as time progresses, the State is going to lose control in certain areas. But the last area where it will lose control is at the centre, and it is therefore ridiculous to challenge the State in this, its strongest area.

One foresees a series of *ad hoc*, decentralised challenges targeted at points of greater State vulnerability, rather than some highly visible, centrally planned opposition that can be crushed relatively easily, and its leaders jailed or restricted. With any centrally planned, mass mobilisation drive the easiest thing for the State to do is to infiltrate and pick up the leadership. Nevertheless, an analysis of the dynamics of the changes and the weak spots, where there inevitably has to be a relinquishing of control, will reveal the areas where people can become more autonomous.

It is not as dramatic or as sensational as a direct challenge but the State has all the resources at its disposal to crush such a challenge. It may be possible to revive what the 17 proscribed organisations had stood for but it would be self-delusionary to think one could simply create new organisations and carry on as before. Equally, if the Provision of Orderly Internal Politics Bill is passed and foreign funding is cut off, a whole range of organisations simply will not survive.

These events have resulted in a kind of strategic realism being forced on extra-parliamentary opposition, demanding that they take some pretty tough decisions.

Ironically, Parliament itself is going to be increasingly unable to mediate in this conflict because the very process that took away the powers from the extra-parliamentary organisations, eroded the constitutional significance of Parliament. As the State took away those powers, accountability in Parliament was also taken away and laid at the door of an extra-parliamentary executive.

The Executive, by increasingly circumventing Parliament, has staged a quiet coup on its own over the past five years. Areas that were traditionally associated with civilian government just do not exist any more. At the same time there has been a loss of ideological purpose. Apartheid was essentially a pro-active ideology – a certain goal was established and those who hated it, could challenge it. But now, apartheid is a reactive ideology – total onslaught and total strategy – and the issue is control.

The issue now is not *when* apartheid is going to collapse or when separate development is not going to work. It has become a logistical exercise: when is the security establishment not going to be able to exercise control?

Now that the State has taken to arguing that a variety of legal activities help fuel the 'revolutionary climate', which opportunities do ordinary citizens have left in a fight for, say, a non-racial democracy? The conventional kind of liberal space in a democratic society does not exist here. The opportunities for protest, marching or voicing one's displeasure are extremely proscribed. The worst thing to do is to treat the South African situation as a civil rights struggle, which it is not. It is a struggle for power, and in that struggle for power or control, the space that people want, they will have to create.

That is why the system that may work here is more likely to be of an Eastern European nature – more like Poland than the USA or a former British colony. South Africa is moving towards the Eastern European totalitarian model where an alternative society develops outside the official structures. As the State deregulates – or privatises – people will start to organise their own lives in their own way.

This slow process of change, this flat-earth view that South African society has been burdened with for four decades, must eventually disappear. Many of us may not live to see it, but there is no need to despair about the future. But what is necessary, is that those who really are committed to a non-racial South Africa will manage to rid themselves of in-fighting, grandstanding and of personalising the struggle.

10

WHAT NEXT OUT OF AFRICA?

Simon Jenkins

Any outsider asked to analyse South African politics puts his reputation at risk. Abroad, having even a passing knowledge of the subject is like suffering from an illness, which requires a lengthy quarantine before the sufferer is accepted back into polite intellectual company. In South Africa itself, analysis is not much easier. For years, South Africans would plead with outsiders: 'See us as we are, not as you would like us to be.' When I first began visiting here in the late 1970s, I laboured to be sympathetic to this admirable admonition, to study the shifting distribution of power and not the distribution of moral rectitude in Southern Africa. Invariably on returning home, I would meet the cry, 'How dare you be objective about apartheid! How dare you waste breath on analysis when you should use it to condemn!'

The task was made more difficult by the overwhelming need to play the prediction game. This required learning a new political language to gauge where South Africa stood on the spectrum of stability versus change. The same promise, the same law, the same speech, the same reform would be presented in starkly different garb to a Western journalist, from that presented to a Nationalist audience. Foretelling the future was like wandering in fog. 'South Africa is changing,' the government said. But to what extent? For the worse or for the better? The concept of reform, ingrained in Botha's nationalism, was wholly opaque. Was it partial reform as a prelude to greater reform or the reverse, a way of forestalling greater reform? Was it unstoppable change or merely the evolution of neo-apartheid? By declaring one's enthusiasm for reform – by 'taking part in the debate' – was one declaring for true democracy or just playing the game of an entrenched regime?

I know these questions have vexed South African liberals for years. But the country's emergence from the trauma of 1985–86 – when a revolutionary scenario enjoyed a brief vogue – has given them new relevance. The impassioned promises of some in government to 'negotiate constitutional change with the blacks' have put even hardened cynics on their mettle. Power-sharing is the buzz-word. Federalism and consociationalism and fancy franchises and blocking thirds are up for grabs. 'Lines are out' to black leadership. Hope is on the agenda once more.

Now we outsiders have a different problem. 'Don't tell us how you think we are,' says the South African. 'We are ready to be told how we ought to be. Those prescriptive spectacles we asked you to smash five years ago ... put them on again. Away with Machiavelli. Give us Bentham and John Stuart Mill. Be constructive, not analytical. Give the reform process the benefit of the doubt. We are weary of *realpolitik* and hungry for idealism.'

I am afraid this chapter will not answer to that yearning. It is stuck in the old ways, in the search for how power is distributed and how it is likely to be in the future. It is in the descriptive, not the prescriptive, mode. It is wary of the naturalistic fallacy.

THE FAILURE OF A CAMPAIGN

From outside, the single cardinal fact of the past two years in South Africa is the failure of external pressure and of internal disturbance to undermine seriously the country's political economy. Although it is easy to paint any economy in black and white terms, few could argue that the sanctions campaign of 1986–87 has contributed either to the emphatic end of apartheid or to the downfall of the white government. If anything, it has merely entrenched the Nationalist government in a belief in its own invulnerability to outside pressure.

That said, the inability of sanctions to show early results is unlikely to lead to their relaxation, probably the reverse. Those arguing for 'another turn of the screw' will continue to enjoy an ascendancy at the UN, in the Commonwealth and within the US Congress. They will be assisted by domestic protectionist lobbies, for instances over coal, iron and fruit imports. On the other hand, the scope for new trade sanctions will become ever more limited and their impact on the South African economy will diminish as political embargoes are overwhelmed by other influences on the terms of South African trade – notably movements in the exchange rate and gold price. Import substitution and sanctions-busting measures will also lessen the impact of sanctions.

It is hard to believe there will by any serious new pressure on the debt front or through restrictions on trade-related banking services. New economic constraints are likely to be directed less through trade or finance and more through a stepping up of pressure to disinvest foreign holdings. This disinvestment has proved the most significant element in South Africa's overseas economic relations in the past two years. As a policy, it is comparatively easy to implement and monitor and is an overt, symbolic act. The corporate sector will still find it the line of least resistance when faced with lobby pressure.

The internal impact of this disinvestment is increasingly counter-productive. It feeds political xenophobia on the right. Where asset disposal is orderly and where franchising and leasing agreements are reached with former South African subsidiaries, even the commercial impact is minimal.

Nonetheless, it is likely that symbolic disinvestment will continue to be a major factor in world policy towards South Africa. The result will be to 'de-colonialise' South Africa's economy even further, to increase self-sufficiency and reduce the impact of further sanctions.

On the non-economic front, there seems little hope of the various sporting, cultural and diplomatic boycotts being relaxed. Even for those who have despaired of economic sanctions, these boycotts retain a simple appeal, sustaining the appearance of 'doing something about apartheid'. At the same time, embargo exemption, granted by the ANC to sympathetic foreign artists and academics, is likely to increase. The longevity of South Africa's isolation will lead to cracks around the edges of ostracism. International foundations and charities will use black contacts to penetrate South Africa's professional, academic and cultural life. The overseas black community will establish acceptable bridgeheads.

For all these reasons, I would expect both economic and non-economic isolation to lose appeal as the central weapon against apartheid. While this does not imply the converse – relaxation of existing embargoes – I sense that a new sort of engagement will become more prevalent. This engagement will also be fuelled, if not by a deeper understanding of events south of the Limpopo, then at least by a deeper awareness of their complexity, which is subsequently discussed.

BETTER THE POLECAT YOU KNOW ...

In the next few years, a significant element in the world's attitude to South Africa will be the rush of other countries to compete in the 'polecat league'. Already this year, we have seen the international media filled with comparisons between Gaza and Soweto. Last year, the constitution imposed by coup in Fiji was compared with that of South Africa, while events in India, Sri Lanka, the Middle East and numerous African States have pushed South Africa's political troubles into the background. This may be a grim way of looking at a country's political image, but the worse the rest of the world behaves, the less awful the 'devil we know'.

Inter-communal strife is nowadays one of the most important elements in international politics. States that have shaken off colonial rule seem to have experienced a brief, euphoric honeymoon before finding themselves torn by the same internal discord from which that rule had given them some relief. The chief casualty of this phenomenon has been one man one vote democracy, the final gift to the Third World of most departing colonial regimes. Such democracy has failed, time and again, to supply stable government to societies divided by ethnicity or religion. One-party rule, militarism or Marxism have all proved more appealing, and more lasting, models for those struggling to hold together disparate communities. In

India, Sri Lanka, Fiji, Cyprus, Ulster, Zimbabwe, Lebanon, Israel, diverse groups have found it impossible to live alongside each other without conflict bursting beyond politics into often persistent violence, bringing with it repression and the erosion of human rights.

Integral to understanding this conflict is that inter-communal strife often demonstrates an immunity to materialism. Group self-interest has to do with cohesion and access to the levers of State power, not crude prosperity. (Note the failure of Israel's policy of economic carrots for the Palestinian refugees.)

The sanctions campaign against South Africa was itself founded on the belief that 'money will ultimately talk', that there is a cost that can be imposed on apartheid which the whites will sooner or later be unwilling to pay. Even on the assumption that this is true, it is unlikely to be more true for the whites than for other ethnic groups. It is said that the whites 'have more to lose' than the blacks and must therefore be more susceptible to declining standards of living. But it is an argument that patently cuts both ways – those who have more to lose, have more to defend.

Black South African support for sanctions is rooted in this confusion: that blacks will willingly impoverish themselves in the cause of their struggle, yet whites will not. Most students of South African politics judge that the whites would probably accept a drastic reduction in their standard of living rather than concede unitary black rule, or even the risk of it. At what point on an ascending scale of violence white intolerance of material self-sacrifice passes black intolerance of the same is, of course, the overriding question. But in matters of communal strife, it is best to start with an assumption that every group is every bit as dedicated to its definition of 'group survival' as another.

As Hermann Giliomee has pointed out (see chapter 2) both white and black South Africans are engaged in a classic inter-group war for the right to control territory – not in some Marxist class struggle over material wealth. It is a characteristic of such conflicts that both sides may endure extremes of loss, deprivation and discomfort rather than give in. I personally believe this perception is crucial in assessing the likelihood of a radical shift away from white domination in South Africa – another way of saying that such change is extremely unlikely in the foreseeable future, whatever the probable cost of resisting it.

This in turn means the outside world will become steadily more acustomed to low-intensity conflict in South Africa. It will realise, of necessity, that many countries are communities at war with themselves and will recognise that these conflicts are not susceptible to easy resolution: indeed, that many are inherently irresolvable.

COLLAPSE OF THE CRISIS MODEL

Time, in this context, is not the great healer, but it is at least a great educator.

Temporal metaphors have become the curse of studies on South African politics. They have come to obscure analysis of the shifts – or lack thereof – in the internal balance of power. The concept of 'time running out' injects an objective urgency which I believe is fallacious and may distort not just prediction but prescription. Since it is constantly used as a guide to policy – notably in Washington – it can merely raise, then dash, expectations.

Equally unreliable is the concept of 'intolerability'. Observers coming afresh to these conflicting communities – Ulster, Cyprus, Lebanon, Kashmir, Israel, South Africa – usually do so with a preconceived notion that the existing state of affairs is so intolerable that it not only must soon end but can only be replaced by an improvement. From this, it is a short step to positing a set of solutions to resolve the conflict 'if only' those involved were prepared to exchange intransigence for flexibility. Those sustaining the status quo are portrayed as 'lunatics' who have lost touch with their own best interests and are doomed to early demise. They are perceived as being not just immoral, but stupid.

In my experience, the benefit of the doubt in the tactics of self-preservation should go to those groups who have showed a capacity to hold onto power against the odds for a period of time. They are likely to be the best judge, if not of their nation's interest, at least of their group's best chances of survival. They are likely (though not invariably so) to have advanced along the learning curve to the point where each shift in the strength of forces against them can be answered with a shift in the compromises, the covert and overt alliances, the chicanery, by which they retain power. What was regarded as an inevitable crisis begins to seem infinitely postponeable. The apocalypse never arrives. Indeed, there comes a point where the conflict inherent in communal diversity appears to establish a sort of wobbly equilibrium. The nuclear reaction never 'goes critical'.

Certainly, it is a feature of intra-national conflicts that they are far longer-lasting than any passing observer thinks possible. Suspended constitutions, states of emergency, external policing operations, *de facto* partitions, low-intensity wars are always greeted as strictly temporary (even Britain's Prevention of Terrorism Act, once regarded as illiberal and draconian). In time, they spin on into the weave of history.

The British province of Ulster has experienced probably more assiduous constitution-mongering than any other political community in the world. Today, the wisest heads are resigned to the conclusion that it is best to assume that this conflict will continue indefinitely: any initiative aimed at bringing the two sides together will be dismissed by the extremists on both sides. Worse, these extremists derive their political elixir from defeating 'moderate' attempts at constitutional compromise, especially attempts at formal power-sharing between political and religious foes. In Ulster, every attempt at inter-group settlement has instigated a literally murderous destabilisation, sent moderates into hiding and brought demagogues howling from the backwoods. Better to establish a security umbrella and hope that in the long term a sort of gradual reconciliation would take place, with a measure of tacit power-sharing accepted outside the context of high-profile political action.

CONCLUSION

This is not to show complacency in the face of totalitarianism or of bloodshed and violence. It is merely to reflect that the forces keeping powerful groups in power need respectful study – as respectful as the forces seeking to topple them – if analysis is not to be doomed to irrelevance. This applies most of all to those of us brought up in the optimistic post-war era and schooled to regard a pluralist democracy as the ultimate in constitutional virtue.

Such democracy is difficult enough to sustain in sophisticated European societies. Experience suggests it is utopian in Third World communities subject to intense group conflict and socio-economic stress. Peaceful constitutional innovation has a poor track record as a way of resolving group conflict. This is especially true on a continent apparently in the process of transferring its constitutional favours from a failed Marxism to a rigorous 'one-party' rule, which means, in essence, rule by the military. Even this transfer is usually achieved by coup rather than by a true revolution.

In these circumstances, constitution-building can be no more than a game played by a regime with its intellectual critics, like a jailor playing chess with his prisoners to distract them from their plight. Negotiations are offered to those out of power, settlements discussed, reassurances given, 'doors kept open'. But until such a regime has an overwhelming reason for surrendering control of events to any or all of its opponents, it is unlikely to risk those negotiations becoming meaningful. We are told that Afrikanerdom does now have such a reason: moral discomfort at its group dominance. We are told that the mechanisms of white rule – mechanisms which include a relentless internal debate – are now being readied for a sharing of power, for a 'great experiment'. I, for one, do not believe it. From my observation, South Africa is no more likely to witness a more than cosmetic shift in its fundamental power structure than it was ten or twenty years ago. Bluntly put, the ruling group does not need it and need not risk it. But at this point, the foreigner decently retires the stage. If South Africa is once again to cheat history, defy experience and amaze the rest of the world, it would not be the first time that the world had read South Africa wrong.

11

THE PROSPECTS OF ACCOMMODATION IN COMMUNAL CONFLICTS: A COMPARATIVE STUDY

Theodor Hanf

It would be quite misleading to interpret and use results of particular comparative studies as a reliable basis for predictions in analogous situations. The number of existing as well as former States for which we have sufficiently reliable data from which to draw relevant conclusions is quite small. Furthermore, perfect analogies between political systems, either in the past or in the present, do not exist. But comparison can help us to ask questions which are relevant to a concrete historical situation; or, better still, to discover certain mechanisms which operate under specific analogous conditions. Best of all, it may enable us to develop an ideal typology, i.e. some system of social and political coordinates that will enable us to record societal realities more accurately.

With these reservations in mind, we shall study a number of past and current conflicts of an entirely or partially communal nature, and try to draw tentative conclusions about their outcome and, especially, the prospects of their accommodation, i.e. their peaceful regulation.

Demarcations from one-dimensional concepts of communal conflict

One distinction may seem obvious. The comparative approach will deal with neither inter-State conflicts nor class conflict within culturally homogeneous States. Rather, its subject is conflict within States in which at least one party to the conflict defines itself not only in terms of economic categories, but in terms of real or perceived cultural differences, such as origin, language, religion, etc.

For the social scientist this is a battlefield, both academically and politically. On the one side are the ethnic 'primordialists', for whom tribes, people, culture, kinship ties and emotional bonds are the stuff from which history is made. On the other side is that group for whom everything the primordialists hold dear is but a by-product of economic interests and contradictions, i.e. 'false consciousness'.

To my mind, the empirical evidence that ethnicity can be created, manipulated and abolished speaks eloquently against primordialism. On the other hand, should ethnicity be 'false consciousness', then both in modern history as well as in our own times far more people have been politically mobilised by 'false' than by 'true' consciousness, have fought and been prepared to die for it.

But there is an even more fundamental objection to both schools of thought. Why should social conflict be considered in predominantly one-dimensional terms – be it horizontal economic conflict between interests 'above' and 'below', or cultural conflict between different vertically juxtaposed groups?

Classical sociology has borrowed the geological term 'stratum'. But as a rule, mountain ranges do not consist only of strata but also of clefts – not every landscape is even. And besides culturally very homogeneous societies there are also culturally cleaved societies, which are both stratified and cleaved. To analyse such societies it is advisable to use at least a two-dimensional approach.

The presence of either distinctive economic or cultural features on their own is insufficient for the emergence of groups whose behaviour is directly conditioned by such characteristics. Karl Marx drew the significant distinction between 'class in itself' and 'class for itself'. The prerequisite for the latter is self-awareness, a product of consciousness. The same is true of cultural distinctions. A society may appear differentiated in terms of any number of objective cultural characteristics, but any group within it emerges as a politically active collective subject only when it perceives itself as distinct from others in terms of one or more cultural characteristics and acts upon this perception, i.e. when it develops a group consciousness. Then it is useful, by analogy to the Marxian concept, to define a 'cultural group for itself' as a 'community'.

Just as the existence of classes 'for themselves' is a prerequisite for class conflict, so is the existence of communities, which consciously perceive themselves as groups with specific interests, a prerequisite for communal conflict.

Thus, in order to analyse conflicts one must first establish whether a society contains both classes and communities as self-conscious groups. Should this be the case, the next, and crucial, question concerns their mode of incorporation. One can distinguish between two ideal types of incorporation: equal or non-ranked, and unequal or ranked. In the former type the lines dividing stratum and class ideally run parallel through all communities. In the latter type, certain communities are ideally identical with classes. But in real societies the ideal type is rare and overlapping boundaries of varying degrees is the rule. Careful study of the mode of incorporation is a prerequisite for any concrete analysis of conflict.

Although the view is widely held that extremely unequal incorporation carries the greatest potential for conflict, there is both empirical and theoretical evidence to the contrary. It has been empirically established that such unequal incorporation can be extraordinarily stable – one may recall Pierre van den Berghe's definition of the Indian caste system as 'apartheid after a thousand years'.

Theoretical reservations are raised by insights into the theory of revolution, largely based on the experiences of culturally relatively homogeneous societies. Conflict tends to erupt after periods of economic improvement among the lower classes, when expectations of further progress are disappointed.

Conflict in multi-communal societies also seems less frequent in cases of predominantly non-ranked or ranked incorporation than in cases of change in the also-existing mode of incorporation. By the same token, conflict is also likely to intensify when communities that have enjoyed class privilege are threatened with loss of privilege. In short: deprivation can be relative not only between strata and classes but also between communities.

However, one may not ignore the general tendency in multi-communal societies for conflict to be expressed as communal rather than as class conflict. There are several reasons for this.

The first is organisational: communal markers facilitate mobilisation. The appeal to what is known and immediately comprehensible – such as ethnic, religious or linguistic affiliation – usually requires a lower level of consciousness than does a sense of class solidarity. To create the latter it is necessary to transcend community feeling, which presupposes an insight into often complicated economic relationships.

A second reason lies in the frequent overlapping of class and communal affiliations. It is often advantageous for the lowest strata of generally privileged communities to align themselves with their community's privileged position as a whole, which accords them a higher social status.

The third – and perhaps the most important – reason for relatively frequent communal conflicts is symbolic deprivation. When people feel themselves despised on account of their ethnicity, religion or language – regardless of their economic status – it inevitably produces bitterness conducive to conflict: though one may not overlook the fact that cultural handicaps almost inevitably have economic consequences.

In summary, conflict patterns in multi-communal societies are more complex than in homogeneous societies. It is often easy to separate economic and cultural aspects of conflict for purposes of analysis, but not in the reality of political experience. Class conflicts in such societies are just as real as in homogeneous societies. But the overlap with communal conflicts, and the latter's more basic and therefore greater mobilisation potential, may conceal class cleavages while at the same time deepening them – a phenomenon 'primordialists' tend to overlook. Supporters of economic monocausality, on the other hand, conveniently ignore a quality peculiar to many communal conflicts: they are often most intense between groups with similar economic status, and may even precipitate economic conflict.

One of the most firmly established empirical findings of conflict studies is the fact that class conflicts are easier to regulate than conflicts between ethnic, religious or linguistic groups. The former are perceived as a matter of 'more or less', of divisible goods; the latter as a matter of 'all or nothing', of indivisible goods, of principle.

Are there any possibilities of accommodating conflicts involving communal elements? The writings of two early Austro-Marxists, Renner and Bauer, provide a useful starting-point.[1] Already at the turn of the century they observed that it was futile to wish away conflicts between nationalities and ethnic groups. But they did think it was possible to depoliticise communal conflicts. The way to set about this was by recognising and institutionalising cultural rights for all groups who perceived themselves as distinct – and by creating as much equality of economic opportunity as possible. Or to use the above terminology: accommodation through equal modes of incorporation. We shall return to this below.

Historical and contemporary examples of accommodating conflicts with strong communal components

Renner and Bauer's medicine came too late to save the patient it was intended for, the Austro-Hungarian Empire, where a practicable form of accommodation was devised only after a civil war and involvement in World War II.

This is not the only case of communal conflict in which peaceful and democratic forms of conflict regulation have not been given a chance. Does this militate against giving them serious consideration? A comparative study of different forms of conflict regulation may help provide an answer to this question.

In this section we shall analyse forms of conflict regulation and their results in a number of historical and contemporary cases of conflict with strong communal components. The choice of cases is largely a reflection of available sources, and may not always be representative of such conflicts. But the size as well as the geographic and cultural spread of the sample is large enough to substantiate hypotheses for the prospects of accommodation of the different modi.

Just a quick glance at Table 1 opposite is enough to draw two important conclusions: (i) there is no 'typical' form of conflict regulation; the results are widely scattered; (ii) the largest category, more than one-quarter of the total, is that of non-regulation, i.e. of unresolved violent conflict. In almost all these cases violence has continued for over a decade – even non-regulation can become a relatively permanent state.

Another quarter of the cases are characterised by one-way conflict regulation: stable or unstable domination of one group over others. There is only

Table 1 Intra-state conflict with strong communal elements

Forms of regulation	I	II	III	IV	V	VI	VII	VIII
Cases reviewed								
AFRICA								
Burundi	x							
Cameroon		x						
Ethiopia				x				
Mali Federation					x			
Rwanda						x		
Sudan				x				
Chad		x						
Uganda				x				
ASIA								
Burma				x				
Union of India			x					
Indonesia						x		
Malaysia					x			
Philippines				x				
Sri Lanka				x				
EUROPE								
Austria							x	
Belgium								x
Holy Roman Empire							x	
German Empire		x						
N. Ireland				x				
Yugoslavia							x	
United Kingdom of the Netherlands					x			
Netherlands								x
Sweden					x			
Switzerland							x	
MIDDLE EAST								
Cyprus			x					
Egypt	x							
Iraq				x				
Jordan		x						
Lebanon				x				
Palestine		x						
Syria		x						
Turkey	x							
	3	6	2	9	4	2	4	2

I   Stable domination
II Unstable domination
III Partition after violence
IV Ongoing war or violence
V Pre-emptive partition
VI One-way accepted accommodation
VII Accommodation after violence
VIII Pre-emptive accommodation

one case of lasting – centuries-old – stable domination: that of Egypt, where a Muslim majority of over 80 per cent has tolerated the Coptic minority, but discriminated against it in innumerable ways. A second case, that of Turkey, is also characterised by an overwhelming Muslim majority, the result of the genocide and expulsion of the Armenian minority. One could regard this as regulation by elimination, and hence homogenisation. In Turkey there are also conflicts involving other minorities: the Kurds, the Shiite Halevis and the Syrian Christians, none of whom are recognised as minorities and therefore subject to enormous pressure to assimilate. A third case of relatively stable dominance is that of Burundi, where the Tutsi minority (14 per cent of the population) has ruled the Hutu majority for centuries. After a revolt in 1973 the Tutsi ascendancy was maintained only by a massacre of about 5 per cent of the population.

The precondition for stable domination appears to be either a huge majority or the extensive use of violence.

However, a number of other cases show that violence on a large scale does not necessarily produce stable domination. Syria is a borderline case. Since the 1960s the Alawites, a 10 per cent minority, have been able to retain power in the face of frequent insurrections and attempted *coups d'état* only by reacting with extreme repression. In Cameroon the Christian-animist South has broken the ascendancy of the Islamic North, while in Chad years of civil war had the opposite effect. In neither case is there any certainty that the current power relationships will persist. In Jordan the monarchy retains power with the support of the Bedouin population, but the Palestinian majority has questioned its legitimacy for decades. In 1970 the monarchy survived only by sending in the army to crush an overt Palestinian challenge. In the territory under Israeli control, the Jewish Israeli majority is increasingly threatened by demographic developments, as well as by uprisings in the occupied territories.

An interesting historical case is that of the German Empire. The civil war of 1866 excluded Austria, thereby reducing the Catholics to a minority. The rulers of the new state expressly perceived it as a Protestant empire. However, Bismarck's attempt to isolate the minority politically through the *Kulturkampf* failed. Only when the Weimar Republic extended the general franchise to Prussia, could Catholics obtain an adequate share of power.

In six case-studies, conflicts between communities have been regulated by partition. In two cases, namely in India and Cyprus, partition took place on the battle-field, after enormous casualties in fighting, massacres and expulsions. In both cases stability is only relative.

In terms of communal criteria, four States have been peacefully partitioned: the Federation of Mali dissolved itself, Singapore separated from Malaysia, and, further back in history, the Union of Sweden and Norway was dissolved and Belgium withdrew from the United Kingdom of the Netherlands. In all four cases there had been little geographical coexistence between the respective communities: the ethnic or religious groups which hived off lived in clearly demarcated territories and had their own traditions and history.

In two case-studies, a majority-initiated one-way accommodation has accorded the minority communities considerable rights. In Rwanda a successful Hutu revolt against the minority Tutsi in 1959–60 broke the long ascendancy of the latter. For over a decade the minority tried to regain power several times, to which the majority just as frequently responded with new repressive measures. In 1973 the Second Republic was established, which granted the minority considerable social and political rights of co-determination under a strict system of proportional ethnic representation. As a consequence, inter-ethnic relations have improved enormously.

In Indonesia the Muslims, above all the Javanese Muslims, form the great majority of the population. The policies of the power centre towards the ethnic, religious and regional minorities have two characteristic features: on the one hand, unconditional rejection and ruthless suppression of each and every separatist tendency, and, on the other hand, obliging and understanding consideration of minorities which accept a united Indonesia without reservation. Within the legal and political framework of a strongly centralised State 'cooperative', minorities enjoy *de facto* federalism, or even a type of consideration which allows consensus in decision-making. This policy of accommodation is facilitated by a political ideology of 'unity in diversity', to which we shall return below.

Conflict regulation in the form of compromise by mutual agreement between the communities involved has taken place in six of the case-studies. In four cases accommodation was reached only after long and bloody wars: in Austria after the civil war of 1934 and association with German defeat in World War II and in Yugoslavia also after World War II. In Switzerland the foundations of the present consociative democracy were laid after the civil war of 1848.

One of the most interesting historical cases is that of the Holy Roman Empire. The Thirty Years' War, in which over one-third of the population died, was ended by the Treaty of Westphalia in 1648. It established a system of power-sharing with numerous checks and balances between the confessions and between the emperor, princes and city-states. This system guaranteed extensive civil rights, a purely defensive foreign policy and a period of relative stability and peace which endured for more than one-and-a-half centuries.

Finally, in two cases compromise of a consociative nature was negotiated as a preventative regulation of potential conflict: the Dutch *pacificatie* of 1917 and the process of constitutional reform in Belgium since the 1960s.

One-quarter of all cases are protracted, bitter and continuing violent conflicts. One-way regulation through domination by one group has huge social costs and is seldom stable. Negotiated solutions have been reached in less than half the cases, and in half of these the result was partition – the mutual recognition that peaceful coexistence was impossible.

Most cases of coexistence through compromise were preceded by bloody struggles. There are few cases of enlightened one-way regulation and other preventative approaches.

Modes of conflict regulation and ideologies of legitimation

The overall pattern of outcomes of conflict described above does not necessarily provide a basis for predictions in specific instances. Therefore it is more important to explain why one or another mode of conflict regulation eventuates. The first step is to investigate whether there is any connection between ideologies articulated and applied to legitimise specific positions in communal conflict, on the one hand, and certain modes of regulation, on the other hand.

To do this, the empirically established ideologies need to be reduced to their essential patterns and categorised.

In very few of our case-studies can the ideological expressions of conflict be explained in terms of the ever-popular social Darwinist patterns, i.e. that any power struggle between two or more obviously different groups – be they called tribes, peoples, national states or nations – is governed by the principle of 'might is right'.

In many cases the question of just what constitutes such a group, indeed whether it exists at all or should exist, is the crux of the matter. The stronger this form of perception – both self-perception and perception by others – the more strongly it is believed. The more strongly a particular perception claims to be the exclusive truth, the more difficult it becomes to regulate conflict.

In this section we shall outline three ideal types of ideological interpretation which together cover virtually all our case-studies.

The first type is Jacobinism. During the French Revolution the Jacobin club formulated and instrumentalised the purest and most radical expression of the principle of *égalité*. Equality was to be understood not only in social but also in cultural terms. Not only were all differences in class and property to be levelled, but all forms of cultural differentiation as well.

The republic was to be *une et indivisible*, centrally administered, unilingual and free of any particularisms. The old French provinces were abolished and replaced by nearly uniform departments. A uniform system of education was introduced to eradicate minority dialects and languages. Ernest Rénan coined the classic formula for cultural and political Jacobinism: the nation is the decision of a daily plebiscite. Expressed negatively, Jacobinism means the abolition of everything in the way of cultural and political equality and unity; expressed positively, the creation of one, indivisible nation by a sheer act of will.

In the 20th century, Jacobinism has become Europe's leading political export, usually sold as 'nation-building': the less homogeneous the social realities in a country, the greater the attraction of a crusade against tribalism, parochialism, particularism and separatism. There is a growing tendency internationally to equate the population of a sovereign territory with 'nation' – which in its original sense means people of the same origins. Yet, the Charter of the United Nations (sic) in contrast to that of its precedessor, the League of Nations, makes the barest of provision for the protection of minorities. In short: Jacobinism is entrenched above all in the Third World.

The second type is ethnic nationalism. In contrast to Jacobinism, it is not voluntaristic but deterministic. Membership of a nation is not based on an act of will, but on fate: history, origins, language and culture are, as it were, natural forces which bind a person to his people, his nation. Ethnic nationalism treats these two concepts as synonymous. Its emergence is closely bound up with language and cultural movements and, above all, the respective historicisms which give each nationalism its ideological character. Whereas Jacobinism seeks nations for existing States, ethnic nationalism seeks States. For communalism, be it ethnic, religious or linguistic, is in the last instance nothing but an ethnic nationalism which has not yet attained its goal, its own State.

Ethnic nationalism did not arise in Western but in Central and Eastern Europe and the Near East, in the territories of the disintegrating supranational Christian and Islamic empires of the 19th century. It too made its way to the Third World. Ethnic nationalism was initially the driving force of anticolonial liberation movements in colonial territories with homogeneous societies. In recent decades, however, it has been enjoying a renaissance in culturally non-homogeneous states in which nation-building is still incomplete and the promise of future unity at the time of independence has remained a fond hope.

Whereas Jacobinism often became the ideology of the new ruling groups and classes, ethnic nationalism in its diverse communalistic forms frequently served as an efficient opposition ideology. Mobilisation of the have-nots and those discriminated against often assumed communalistic forms in opposition to other communities perceived as privileged.

A third type may be termed syncretistic nationalism. Its goal is also nation-building, but, unlike Jacobinism, not from scratch. Instead, existing organic cultural units are seen as building blocks. This approach is usually based on a dual awareness. On the one hand, it is futile to hope that existing communities will simply disappear; yet the social and cultural costs of disrupting them – uprooting, insecurity and the breakdown of social and moral standards – would be too high, or might even provoke insurmountable resistance. On the other hand, in a society in which different communities are not segregated but live and work among one another, radical ethnic nationalism or communalism would be like trying to unscramble the omelette, and would destroy the fabric of the State through resettlements, expulsions, and the like with incalculable economic consequences. Syncretistic nationalism insists neither on unity nor diversity at all costs, but unity in diversity.

It has fathered – again reduced to ideal types – two different approaches to constitutional policies. The first is the institutionalisation of communities, so as to harness communalism in the interests of communal coexistence within an all-embracing nation. This approach is present in certain consociative democracies, but is also reflected, for example, in Lenin's theory of nationalities. The other approach is that which aims to de-politicise communalism: fostering maximal cultural diversity in order to promote political unity, as is being attempted in Canada and Indonesia.

Which roles do these types of ideology play in the forms of conflict regulation we have identified? In the case of stable domination the ruling group tends to insist on the homogeneity of the nation, denying the existence of different communities. Thus, in Turkey the Kurds are called 'mountain Turks'; in Burundi ethnicity is officially held to be a colonial invention.

The situation is similar in some systems of unstable domination. No Arab government professes pan-Arabism more fervently than the Syrian regime, which also denies that the country is ruled by a minority and accuses opposition groups of confessionalist communalism. The Jordanian monarchy presents itself as an impartial authority which does not distinguish between Transjordanians and Palestinians. The governments of Cameroon and Chad, both before and after the respective changes in government, plead the pure Jacobinistic concept of the State, and are sensitive to charges of ethnic favouritism. Israel alone has dispensed with any integrating ideology and pleads a religious claim to the land – not to the country's non-Jewish inhabitants. Accordingly, the principal domestic issue in Israeli politics is the question of whether it is better to cede land because of its inhabitants, or to hold onto this land despite them.

However, most cases of violent conflict are characterised by struggles between Jacobins and ethnic nationalists rather than between competing communalisms. But professions of Jacobinism can mask ethnic aspirations. In the name of a united Burma, Sri Lanka, Iraq, Sudan, Uganda and the Philippines, the respective majorities in power are fighting their non-Buddhist hill people, their Tamils, Kurds, black Christians and animists, Muslim minority, and in the last case everyone else. In the Lebanon the Shiites discovered Jacobinism when they believed they had become the largest ethnic group, while in Northern Ireland the Protestants and Catholics at times wear alternative Jacobin cloaks – that of the United Kingdom and that of the United Republic of Ireland.

The cases of partition, as mentioned above, demonstrate the view that both domination and coexistence are impossible.

Finally, in cases of negotiated as well as one-way accommodation, different types of syncretistic nationalistic ideologies dominate. If accommodation is preceded by armed conflict, communalism tends to become politically institutionalised, as in Switzerland, Yugoslavia and the former Holy Roman Empire.

Preventative as well as one-way negotiated solutions, however, tend to favour the recognition of existing ethnic, cultural or religious differences with the object of depoliticising them. The Netherlands is politically a centralised State, but education and the media are left to the pluralism of the various communities, often referred to as 'pillars' (*zuilen*). Belgium has transferred all cultural matters and education to the autonomous administrations of the three language groups. Canada subsidises all efforts on the part of any immigrant group to preserve its 'heritage language'. Indonesia decided not to make Javanese – the language of the majority – its official language, introducing instead the *bahasa Indonesia*, which all citizens have to learn as their second language.

It is Indenesia too that has produced a particularly innovative syncretistic national ideology, the *panca sila*, which amalgates belief in one God and confessional equality between Islam, Protestantism, Catholicism, Buddhism and Hinduism with the goals of a welfare State, solidarity, democracy and nationalism, in order to create 'unity in diversity'.

Thus, the three ideal types of legitimising ideologies tend to go hand in hand with different forms of conflict regulation. Why this is so can be explained by different starting conditions and vested interests, to which we turn below.

The rules of the communal game

Community politics, as, indeed, politics *per se*, is about the distribution of power and privilege. In every political system there are different transmissive institutions between the citizens and the political power centre – parties, pressure groups, lobbies, syndicates, etc. In general, the most important intermediary institutions in multi-communal systems are the communities or their political agencies. In contrast to political parties or syndicates in homogeneous societies, among which citizens are free to choose, membership in communities is, as a rule, determined by markers, be they ethnic, religious or linguistic.

Intermediary institutions and membership of them are important for access to power and privilege. This is illustrated most clearly by the spoils system practised in certain Western democracies: immediately after a former opposition party has won an election, hundreds of incumbents in government, administration and often even parastatal enterprises are replaced. What distinguishes multi-communal systems from such Western systems is the fact that access to and exclusion from positions of power and privilege are determined by ascriptive criteria. In other words, successful communalistic power politics brings easy profits. Individuals derive advantages because they belong to a specific community. Conversely, defeat has serious disadvantages.

Interest in communal power politics naturally fluctuates, depending on the social stratum and on phases of economic development. As a rule, interest is greatest among the leadership groups: they have the greatest opportunities to benefit. Those who run the greatest risk of loss are the lower strata of the dominant group. They owe their position of relative privilege not to their own abilities or services, but to their group affiliation. Hence, they are often particularly militant communalists. Successful, upwardly mobile members of the discriminated group frequently form a third critical group. If, notwithstanding ability and achievements, their advancement is influenced by ascribed characteristics, they tend to organise themselves on a communalistic basis – or else to work actively for the abolition of communalistic structures.

What is true of these three critical groups is by no means necessarily true of the population as a whole. Some authors take a Hobbesian view of multi-communal societies – *homo homini lupus*: every community is a wolf pack to the others. Lijphart, for example, works on the assumption that only élite cartels of wise and tolerant leaders can bring the tendentiously hostile masses to accept coexistence.[2] But this begs the question of how hostile and intolerant masses are going to produce such tolerant and open-minded leaders.

But over and above this, there is empirical evidence that even in strongly polarised societies the great majority of the population has a clear perception of common interests and, hence, in principle, the will to coexist. There is much to recommend the view that it is not so much the communities, i.e. the mass of the population, which bear responsibility for communalistic mobilisation and the deepening of cleavages, as the above-mentioned critical groups with vested interests; in other words, the leadership, the upwardly mobile section of underprivileged communities and the section most threatened by loss of group privilege. These critical groups naturally have an overriding interest in identifying with the group interests of the entire community. Consequently, most communal 'entrepreneurs' are recruited from their ranks.

Identification of the critical groups already gives some indication of the specific economic and historical circumstances that are most likely to be conducive to communal mobilisation. 'Pre-modern', in other words pre-industrial and pre-bureaucratic, communal differences are often less laden with conflict. Peasant populations of different communities often live peacefully side by side for centuries. There are also innumerable instances of communal division of labour in urban cash societies occurring without crisis. As already discussed in the first section, critical mobilisation of communalism occurs primarily when previously existing – equal or unequal – modes of class and community incorporation undergo change.

And this is the case above all at times of economic upheaval – the beginnings of industrialization, rapid urbanisation and closer communication between people.

Theories of modernization postulate that industrialization, urbanisation and communication are powerful forces for social integration and would rapidly break down communal loyalties. In practice, the realities of social development in multi-communal societies have for the most part refuted this assumption. Although people from different communities live together in the new cities, they do not necessarily mix. Their contact is for the most part in competing for jobs and posts in industry and the public administration. In this competitive situation they receive assistance and patronage primarily from their immediate compatriots, their fellow tribesmen and fellow speakers, in short: communal support. In the new and strange situations in modern society, as their social relationships undergo radical change, they find stability among members of their own community. But perhaps of even greater importance, they frequently experience inequality, rejection and discrimination as a result of the ascriptive criteria of their community affiliation. Social inequality is a powerful revitaliser of communal solidarity.

In almost all societies with acute communal conflicts one hears that 'in the past' the different communities accepted one another. In most cases this is true, either because the relative equality in peasant societies gave less cause for tension or because differences in the past had been accepted as God-given or ordained by history. With the appearance of industrialization, urbanisation and more intensive communication, tensions increased. Because change appears possible, people want it immediately. In short: as a rule 'modernization' revitalises communalism – or creates it in the first place. Pre-industrial communalism seldom embraced more than clans or regional kinship groups. Modern communalism encourages larger associations: the larger the community, the greater the prospects of success. The critical groups identified above have an interest in gaining as many supporters as possible. The modern society has brought on the hour of communalistic mobilisation.

Communal conflict is primarily about political power. The 'more modern' an economy, the greater is the State's role as an agency distributing power and the consequent privilege.

As a rule, the application of ideologies – communalistic or otherwise – in the struggle for power is thoroughly rational. A study of which ideologies are employed by whom and under what conditions illustrates clearly both the rational and the instrumental nature of ideology: generally it is an intelligible articulation of identifiable communal strategies in pursuit of interests. This is not to doubt that supporters of a certain ideology believe in it, or have commitment and conviction. Obviously, however, it is easy to profess a belief which coincides with one's interests.

There are two fundamental variants in communal politics: in one there are clear majorities and minorities, in the other there are not. In the former, the competing groups prefer strategies of Jacobinistic and communalistic mobilisation respectively. In the latter, these strategies are employed, but groups often also resort to syncretistic nationalism in their attempts to regulate conflict. These two cases will be analysed separately.

Table 2 Ideological strategies in cases of clear majorities and minorities

	Jacobinism	Communal mobilisation
Ruling majority	−	+
Ruling minority	+	−
Dominating majority	+	−
Large dominated minority	−	+
Small dominated minority	+	−

Ruling majorities can afford to rule with the support of their own group alone. By excluding minorities from any share in power, the ruling groups maximise their benefits.

Ruling minorities, by contrast, prefer to disguise the fact of minority rule. Jacobinism is the most suitable ideology to disguise different degrees of privilege, for it avoids symbolic deprivation of the majority, thereby minimising its opposition.

As a rule, dominated majorities also articulate their interests in Jacobinistic terms. The dominated do not demand the replacement of one ascendancy by another, but a new system of equality devoid of discrimination against any group. Were a dominated majority to adopt a strategy of communal mobilisation, the ruling minority would be forced to choose between capitulation or intransigence, which would inevitably stimulate the resolution of the dominated group to resist. A Jacobinistic vision of future equality, on the other hand, also offers some prospects for a minority, which makes it easier for it to consider the loss of exclusive power.

Large dominated minorities, on the other hand, frequently prefer a strategy of communal mobilisation. Their prospects of ever exercising exclusive power are very slight. The better they organise themselves and the more completely they mobilise, the greater their prospects of becoming a 'blocking minority', without whose approval little can be done. Consequently, it becomes worth something to the majority to trade some of its privileges for the cooperation of the minority.

Finally, small dominated minorities almost always prefer Jacobinism. 'If you cannot beat them, join them' would describe their position in a nutshell.

For both well-defined majorities and minorities a rational assessment of their respective interests usually dictates a clear choice of strategy. In most cases the choice is made in accordance with the patterns outlined above.

However, when majorities as well as the power relationships between majorities and minorities are less defined, the conditions are quite different. Both Jacobinistic and communalistic strategies hold potential dangers for both sides. Jacobinism can quickly degenerate into sham equality; and a mobilised community may achieve many of its objectives but also lose something in the process.

As a rule, communities that proclaim Jacobinistic ideals are those that either have or believe they have a slight majority, and for whom majority rule means nothing else but rule by the majority of their own community. Communities in a slight minority seek to avert the perceived danger of permanent exclusion from power by demanding the institutionalisation of communalism. The instrumental function of competing ideologies becomes most apparent when demographic shifts cause the positively and negatively affected communities to exchange their ideological preferences.

In quite a few cases armed conflict is a consequence of miscalculations about the practicability of claims and demands. In these situations the game of communities resembles most closely the classic, prenuclear game of nations. And frequently it is a deadly game in which there are – in the words of Mike Copeland – no winners, only losers.

Nevertheless, multi-communal systems without any clear majority have also found mutually acceptable forms of conflict regulation, and developed syncretistic national ideologies in support of these solutions. Let us consider the conditions conducive to the creation of such forms.

Conditions for negotiated accommodation

Such conditions seldom exist in cases of indisputable domination, as in the case of States which have sustained crushing defeat in international wars: the terms of victory are not negotiated, they are dictated.

The only difference between these and cases of unstable domination is that in the latter the defeated can hope to improve their situation or perhaps even turn the tables at the next opportunity.

But in both groups there are few prospects of serious negotiations as long as one side is in a position to enforce a one-way distribution of power and privilege favourable to itself.

Negotiated solutions are most plausible in situations in which all the groups involved realise that no single group is strong enough to gain a clear victory, yet no group is so weak as to be an obvious loser – in other words, in no-win situations.

Most of the cases studied in which negotiations did take place were preceded by violent, protracted conflicts. Only when all sides had reached exhaustion did they accept that victory was impossible.

Yet, a no-win situation does not in itself guarantee peace – otherwise numerous communal wars would not have dragged on for years, even decades, without any clear outcome. The parties involved must first accept that none of them will or can attain all their material and ideological objectives. A conflict can be ended by mutual consent only if all parties agree to share the country's wealth fairly, to recognise the country's existing cultural diversity and, above all, to renounce their respective 'pure' ideologies, Jacobinistic as well as ethnic-communalistic. It is typical of conflicts of this type that it is often easier to reach a compromise on material than on symbolic and ideological matters.

The clearest illustration of this is the frequent practice of scorched-earth policies. Although such policies are utterly irrational in purely economic terms, they are often adopted by groups in situations of real or imagined threat to their existence. Hence, negotiations can be successful only when the symbolic and ideological prerequisites have been satisfied, when all parties have gained the impression that their existence as a group is no longer threatened.

This is the time of syncretistic national ideologies which accept contradictions, inconsistencies and diversity – a diversity devoid of any claim to a monopoly of power and group privilege.

Against the background of battle the Treaty of Westphalia emerged, midwife to an empire of Catholics, Lutherans and Non-conformists; the 'Lebanese Formula' was devised, which treated 17 Muslim and Christian communities as constituents of a common Lebanon; the Swiss 'magic formula' took shape, which made Helvetians of German-, French-, Italian- and Romansch-speaking Protestants and Catholics; and the Constitution of Socialist Yugoslavia was drawn up, which recognises different peoples united within one nation.

All these solutions are abominations for Jacobins as well as for supporters of an exclusive, ethnic communalism. But the people directly affected have learnt not only to prefer such ideological abominations to the abominations of war, but also to regard them as part of the wealth of their nations – not a measure of last resort but one of their strengths.

The prospects of reaching such solutions without first experiencing the futility of violence are bad. Peoples and societies have a habit of learning not from the history of others but only from their own bloody experience.

Of course there are exceptions to the rule, notably Belgium and the Netherlands, but the significance of their conflicts was comparatively small.

It is questionable whether similar results would eventuate under more difficult conditions.

But empirical probability is not historical certainty by any means. One cannot exclude the possibility that the wisdom of preventative accommodation may also prevail under difficult conditions.

Our two examples of one-way syncretistic nationalism – Rwanda and Indonesia – run counter to established probability. In both cases the numerically and politically overwhelming majority can afford to practise policies which either ignore or discriminate against minorities. Yet neither does. They are evidence that multi-communal societies need not be Hobbesian. They also provide evidence that a no-win situation is not a precondition for syncretistic national ideologies, which can be a free and voluntary choice. This at least warrants the attempt at ideological engineering in difficult situations.

This brings us back to our point of departure. The business of politics in general and of multi-communal societies in particular is power and privilege. If power and wealth are unequally distributed the consequence is either domination – latent conflict – or open conflict. Negotiated, mutually agreed and, hence, legitimate accommodation is possible only if domination and privilege are lessened. A syncretistic national ideology may serve this purpose. Whether one views syncretism negatively, as diluted, inconsistent and messy, or positively, as complex, imaginative and comprehensive, it has one particular characteristic of inestimable value in complex societies that Jacobinism and ethnic nationalism lack: tolerance.

Reflections on the debate on nationalism in South Africa

This concluding section is not an attempt at weighing up the power relationships and future prospects of the political groupings and policies currently competing in South Africa. In terms of total population there is a pronounced asymmetry between power and legitimacy in South Africa. The form of regulation obtaining in South Africa is domination. It is an open question whether in terms of our ideal types this domination is still stable or tending towards instability.

Certainly, South Africa is still very far from a no-win situation. In many respects the situation resembles that in Poland. The majority of the population may be rebellious and reject the government, but the government is firmly in power, and neither impressive guerrilla actions nor huge frequent and widespread quasi-insurrectionary demonstrations have been able to alter this fact. Although the government is unable to brainwash the majority of the population, it is well able to prevent behaviour of which it disapproves.

Therefore, at present there is nothing to force the dominating group in South Africa to negotiate. On the other hand, it might prefer to negotiate from a position of relative strength than to risk having to negotiate at a later stage, after power relationships have changed.

The political organisations of the black majority have less choice. For the organisations in exile the question of negotiations is not currently relevant, for the simple reason that the government is not prepared to talk to them. For the organisations within the country the framework for negotiations the government has offered seems so restrictive that it is out of the question for them to accept it.

In short: At present the preconditions for serious negotiations do not exist. The ruling minority does not have to negotiate and the ruled majority does not want to negotiate under the given premises.

This situation will not change until the existing constellation of power has been modified considerably – towards which the organisations in exile are working consistently – or until the definitions of the framework and respective objectives of negotiations have become less incompatible than at present. The initiative lies with the group in power because it *is* in power and it is up to the dominant group to grasp it. The comparative analysis has shown that prophylactic negotiations are rare. Also, in the case of South Africa, it is more than probable that the group in power will refuse to negotiate seriously until it is forced to the negotiating table. On the other hand, the possibility of a negotiated solution cannot be completely excluded, hence it is worthwhile at least to consider the conditions under which such negotiations would be conceivable.

Negotiation is a process and there is little to be gained by speculating about possible results of negotiations until this process is under way. The literature on a future South Africa, the redistribution of its wealth and the sharing and division of power is a library in itself. We do not intend to augment it; our concern is the preparatory stage.

The first question concerns the degree to which the strategies of the conflicting parties encourage or discourage negotiations.

For the best part of a century the strategy of the dominating group has been one of ethnic mobilisation. It was indisputably functional and remarkably successful as long as the supreme goal was power within the exclusively white political system. The system was a parliamentary one, with the Afrikaners forming the majority among the white population. Ethnic mobilisation of this majority was the way to power. The nationalist Afrikaners gained 'white power' in 1948 and have retained it ever since.

But demographically, white South Africa forms only one-sixth of all South Africa and that proportion is decreasing. What was successful for the majority within a minority need not be expedient for a minority against the majority. As discussed above, minority rule is best assured by inclusive, all-embracing strategies – by Jacobinistic ideologies. Nationalist Afrikanerdom has tried to maintain its ascendancy by means of an exclusive, particularistic, ultra-communalistic strategy. Not only did it define itself as a separate people, but it sought to ordain as, and then dominate, specific 'peoples' of a majority which did not want this at all.

This domination has been eroded considerably with time. Minority rule hand in hand with an exclusive ideology presupposes not only that superiority is absolute but also that it is unquestioned. Hendrik Verwoerd was the first white ethnic strategist to grasp the fact that this strategy was untenable in the long run. He opted to abandon crude domination in favour of disguised domination through partition: the 'homeland' policy of sham partition that would not affect the real power relationships. But the ideological erosion had begun. Verwoerd's slogan of 'separate, but equal' did what paternalistic 'baasskap' and the ideology of crude segregation, 'apartheid' did not: regardless of the gap between slogan and reality, it recognised in theory the claim of the dominated majority to equality. Since then, vesting this ideology has become a semantic fashion parade.

In the mid-70s, parallel to sham partition as the 'solution' for the blacks, sham consociation was introduced as the 'solution' for the coloureds and Indians. But they remain sham solutions because they do not affect the central element of domination, viz. one-way conflict regulation. Since the early 1980s new ideological elements have increasingly gained ascendancy, in particular the concept of common security against a 'total onslaught'. To attain this security, the government has offered to 'negotiate' with all dominated population groups. It is self-evident that security in this respect is primarily the security of the ruling group. And it is doubtful whether negotiations under conditions of extremely unequal power relationships can be more than sham negotiations – presuming there are black leaders prepared to take part.

Has this parade from sham partition through sham consociation to sham negotiation been only different ideological vestments of domination, or signals of a changing body as well? Let us examine them more closely. By abandoning its policy of partition, the government signalled its recognition of the impossibility of unscrambling the geographic omelette of the South African population. There is a long road between Connie Mulder's declaration that in future there would be no black South Africans, and PW Botha's proclamation of common citizenship for all South Africans. Previously one spoke of logical 'developments' in an unchanging basic policy; Deputy Minister van der Merwe now speaks of a '180° change in policy'.

Changes at an ideological and symbolic level are perhaps even more significant. The repeal of the Immorality Act and the Mixed Marriages Act has few practical implications for the vast majority of the majority, but the ideological implications for the minority should not be underestimated. The sexual taboo has always been one of the pillars of apartheid ideology, reflecting its pseudo-biological justification. What outsiders may regard as a storm in an Afrikaner teacup is an ideological tidal wave for people who have grown up in a coherent system of racial convictions. Why did the government implement these changes? One can only assume that the leadership increasingly realised that although an exclusive communalistic strategy that does not respect the rights of other groups may have been an effective means of gaining power in the white parliamentary system, it is an increasingly ineffective means of protecting the interests of a minority within a far larger population.

The changing ideological paradigms reflect attempts to find a new, better, more functional strategy that is not *a priori* unacceptable to all other groups, a strategy based on the calculation that 'even if we still can beat them, it might be better to allow them to join us'.

On the other side, among the dominated majority, there are two divergent strategies, the strategy of the African National Congress and the strategy of African nationalists. The ANC's strategy is clearly Jacobinistic, while the Africanists' contains strong elements of communalistic mobilisation.

The Jacobinism of the ANC differs from many other forms of Jacobinism in that decisive elements reflect not so much nationalism *per se* as the universalism of Christian as well as Marxist thought. The goal of absolute equality for all people, which can be realised only in the freedom of all men, is rooted in the concept of the brotherhood of all people. The Christian teaching that God can change the hearts of people – even, and especially, those of oppressors – and Marxist caution against premature revolution may well explain why the ANC pinned its hopes on non-violent change for decades. The knowledge that the great majority of black South Africans are fundamentally peaceful, as well as the disciplined revolutionary cadre's horror of useless and indiscriminate violence, probably explains why the ANC is now striving to keep armed struggle within the narrow bounds of carefully selected 'hard' targets.

Because all South Africans are brothers in the eyes of the ANC, regardless of race, language and ethnicity, its struggle is not against 'the whites' but against the present system which prevents equality and fraternity. Hence the ANC regards without reservation all white South Africans who accept the ANC's ideals as 'part of the struggle'. Even the fact that so far only a negligible number of whites have joined the ANC has not changed this attitude.

This fundamental tolerance towards all individuals has led the ANC to reject radically all forms of group thinking. This was not always the case. The ANC has long been conceived of – and also organised – plurally: based on collaboration between Africans, Indians and whites as different but like-minded groups. It was government policy – the unilateral definition of groups, the manipulation and ascription of ethnicity – that induced the ANC to reject all group formulas, regardless of their nature and reason, as expression and symbol of a system of oppression. Thus today, the ANC wants neither multiracialism, pluralism, consociation, federalism, nor even groups based on voluntary association. It is exclusively concerned with pure *non*-racialism – 'one person, one vote in an undivided South Africa'.

To appreciate fully the extraordinary power of this non-racial ethic one must see it in the context of historical experience – and in that of the personal experience of each black South African. For forty years all aspects of each and every black person's life have been conditioned by imposed group structures. Every white election is renewed evidence that the majority of whites support this policy. In view of this reality, the fact that upholders of the ANC tradition do not regard all whites as enemies must be seen as almost heroic. It is also understandable that any form of communalism should be anathema to them.

Adherents of the Africanistic approach consider it futile to subscribe to such convictions. They share the ANC's ideals but think its strategy wrong. As there are no serious prospects that whites will become allies they see little point in refraining from mobilising the outrage of black Africans. Only when they are free from these illusions will blacks become aware of their own power and liberate themselves without any help or interference from whites. For Africanists a non-racial liberation movement remains no more than a remote ideal. Furthermore, they feel that the collaboration of no more than a handful of whites obstructs rather than helps them find their own feet both politically and organisationally.

The Africanistic approach always strikes a chord with the younger generation which is dissatisfied with the ostensible moderation of the ANC leadership and particularly frustrated by the lack of success of moderate black protest. This was the case in the late 1950s, when the PAC split off from the ANC, as well as in the mid-70s, when the black consciousness movement arose without any organisational links with the older, larger ANC and PAC. There are already indications that the crushing of the UDF, yet another attempt at furthering ANC ideals by peaceful means, will lead to a renaissance of Africanistic ideas.

Notwithstanding this, there can be no doubt that it is the ANC tradition — its concepts, goals and strategy — which continues to shape the political thinking and the attitudes of the great majority of black South Africans.

With changing paradigms within the ruling group and continued adherence to the idea of a united, indivisible South Africa among the larger section of the dominated majority, what is the significance of these ideological and strategic positions for the prospects of conflict regulation by negotiation?

The paradigmatic change is unquestionably an attempt at encouraging the dominated groups to cooperate in devising new forms of coexistence in South Africa. 'No group may dominate another' is indeed a different concept to the domination of a single group, or to partition. Yet, the new formula has not effected any change in the realities of life for the black majority. The dominance of one group is unbroken and is still enforced with a heavy hand; indeed, the hand may even lie heavier. For those affected it makes no difference whether one is gaoled in the name of 'baasskap', of apartheid, of separate development or of security and negotiation. The black majority have too often experienced that the substance of new paradigms is exhausted in the battle of semantics. All too often in the past, solutions presented as new have been sham. What is the use of repealing the Mixed Marriages Act as long as the Population Registration Act and the Group Areas Act are still in force?

What the government is now proposing may in fact be something new, but the majority regards it as shopsoiled goods in fresh wrapping. Past experience, existing conditions and those likely to obtain in the foreseeable future mean that the government lacks the credibility and persuasive power necessary for negotiations.

But what about the persuasive power of the alternative non-racial ideology and its prospects of gaining the support of a substantial section of the minority? There can be little doubt that the ANC type of Jacobinism is theoretically more acceptable to a minority than pan-Africanism. But the attraction of a South Africa with equal rights for all is very limited for a minority interested not only in guarantees for individual rights but also for group rights. For many, above all the Afrikaners, it is a question not only of power and privilege, but of their existence as a group perceived as a separate people and nation.

As discussed earlier, there are examples of groups which have been prepared to forego privilege and exclusive power rather than compromise on conditions they regard as fundamental to their existence as a group.

Already in the late 18th century Dutch settlers had rebelled ostensibly against restrictions imposed on their independence by the Dutch East India Company: 'We are Afrikaners' was the rallying cry. Afrikaners subsequently experienced twice what they, rightly or wrongly, regarded as domination by others: the post-Napoleonic decades of British rule in the Cape Colony and the period after the Anglo-Boer War. They also experienced symbolic deprivation twice in the attempts by the ruling group to assimilate them linguistically and culturally. Precisely this struggle against assimilation gradually forged Afrikaner group consciousness. Once a group consciousness has emerged, it is a political reality. It cannot be ignored, nor will it simply disappear because others think it 'false'. Afrikaner group consciousness proved to be so strong that the conflict between Boer and Brit can still arouse powerful emotions in daily clashes of quite a different nature.

It may be true that at present the preservation of power and privilege conditions Afrikaner group consciousness more than do common bonds of language and culture. But the latter are present, rooted in emotional depths beyond economic and political opportunism, ready to be mobilised.

There are numerous examples of groups which have behaved in a politically and economically irrational way when they perceived a threat to their existence as a group. For centuries Arab Christians and Jews have preferred discrimination and remained Christians and Jews, although they could have achieved equality at any time as Muslims. Kurds are supposed to be Turks, and could easily be so, but obstinately remain Kurds. Québecois and Flemings defy all national economic thinking to retain their languages and customs. In a nutshell, group consciousness can be associated with power and privilege and also with lack of privilege, but can endure even when equal opportunity is open to individuals.

The Jacobin ideology offers the Afrikaners as individuals complete equality if they renounce power and privilege. But it denies the Afrikaners as a group any rights whatsoever. For those with a strong group consciousness the concept of one country for all South Africans is tantamount to unconditional surrender as a group. And such a perception mobilises all sections of the group which perceives itself threatened.

If this is indeed the case then the ideologies of the ruling minority and the subjected majority appear to be totally incompatible and mutually exclusive. This widens a conflict over power and privilege, which is difficult enough to regulate as it is, into a conflict over fundamental convictions and principles, thereby making it even more intractable. Deterministic and voluntaristic nationalisms, exclusive and inclusive concepts, an ethnic appeal to bonds of kinship and history versus a universalistic appeal for equality and fraternity: in each case these differences are irreconcilable. As we saw above, most unregulated violent conflicts exhibit precisely the same cleavages.

What has proved to be the optimal mobilising ideology for each side in the light of their respective historical experiences proves utterly unsuitable as an instrument to persuade the other side. The real load of conflict, already burdened by the huge disparities in power and prosperity, is enormously increased by the fundamental ideological cleavage. Should the acceptance by one side of the other's ideology be raised to a precondition of negotiation, it is very likely that there will never be any negotiation at all – at least, not before one side is victorious and the other defeated.

The last question concerns the possibilities of defusing the ideological conflict, of prophylactic ideological disarmament. Hermann Giliomee has recently suggested forms of possible South African bicommunalism (see Chapter 2). Unhappy historical and contemporary examples such as Cyprus, India and Palestine should give cause for thought. Lijphart regards a face to face confrontation between two communities as an unfavourable condition for conflict regulation. But more importantly, bicommunalism would be conceivable in South Africa only if a majority of the Africanist school of thought were in favour of it. This is neither very probable nor particularly helpful. Even though black nationalism would be easier for Afrikaner ethnic nationalists to understand, black nationalism would hardly be more open to compromise than non-racial nationalism. It would appear that the only plausible way of defusing the current ideological conflict – group thinking versus the rejection of group thinking – lies in both sides giving thought to some form of ideological syncretism.

Is this possible, and what form could it take? On the part of the ruling minority the first point to establish would be whether its prime concern is 'race' or in fact cultural groups. Albeit with some difficulty, Jacobins can live with group differences based on culture and language, whereas they most certainly cannot accept pseudo-biologically defined groups embracing enormous cultural diversity.

The criterion 'white' embraces Afrikaans- and English-speakers, Greeks and Portuguese, Christians and Muslims, i.e. it is not a cultural criterion but one of skin-colour – and one which makes sense only in terms of privilege.

If Afrikaans-medium schools were to admit all children whose mother tongue is Afrikaans and English-medium schools all anglophone children, the desire to retain cultural identity would be far more credible than it is at present.

The distinction between community and race would be a necessary, though not a sufficient step. Groups or communities could become an acceptable criterion and acquire legitimacy only if they are not ordained but voluntarily constituted. Communities become communities only when the people concerned decide that this is what they are. This also implies that people may choose not to belong to any circumscribed community at all. In Yugoslavia, for instance, citizens have the choice of belonging to any one of the various nationalities within the borders of the country or of defining themselves simply as 'Yugoslav'. A community which is secure in its own identity has no cause to fear a system of voluntary affiliation.

Communalism legitimated by voluntary affiliation and not by racial criteria should not be inconceivable for supporters of a non-racial, united South Africa – particularly as it could help to ease the transition away from the present situation.

The renunciation of cultural Jacobinism and a clear affirmation of linguistic and cultural diversity should be conceivable also, and especially, for those whose prime goal is democratic equality and national unity. There are enough examples – from Canada through Switzerland to the Soviet Union – which prove that the recognition of cultural diversity is not an obstacle to the emergence of a strong national identity. Conversely, the examples are legion that cultural Jacobinism unavoidably causes symbolic deprivation, which provokes vehement resistance and the adoption of survival policies.

Recognising cultural diversity is the best means of depoliticising such diversity. The recognition of voluntary cultural communalism accords it a legitimacy which may, in turn, help to lessen its relevance gradually and democratically.

These reflections will certainly not be to the liking of those who support a clear and simple ideology. Clear and simple ideologies are invaluable when one wants to mobilise one's respective supporters – and when one is sure of gaining a clear and indisputable victory. But if one is not, or has good reason to fear the price one's supporters will have to pay for a possible victory, then it is worthwhile thinking about diluted, complicated, syncretistic ideologies.

Whatever the case, ideologies are no more than the software of conflict regulation. They may help to make it easier or more difficult to initiate negotiations. The hardware is power. However, some have lost it and others have failed to gain it because they did not apply the proper strategy.

In some of the cases of conflict we have looked at there are winners and losers, in many only losers. In virtually all cases there are casualties. Those who are concerned about these casualties may feel tempted to think about syncretism. Clear and simple ideologies have little meaning in cemeteries.

NOTES

[1] Bauer O, *Die Nationalitätenfrage und die Zozialdemokratie, Marx Studien Nr 2*, zweite auflage, Vienna: Wienervolksbuchhandlung, 1924.
Renner K, *Das Selbstbestimmungsrecht der Nationen in bezondere anwendung auf Osterreich: Erste Teil: Nation und Staat*, Leipzig/Vienna: Deuticke, 1918.
[2] Lijphart A, *Democracy in Plural Societies*, New Haven: Yale University Press, 1977.

12

THE COMMUNAL NATURE OF THE SOUTH AFRICAN CONFLICT

Hermann Giliomee

INTRODUCTION

As the layers of apartheid peel away, the communal essence of the South African conflict becomes ever more visible. The communal conflict is rooted in the history of the country as a settler colony and the resultant black struggle against a political system dominated after 1948 by Afrikaner nationalists, the core group of the larger white community. The huge gap in material wealth between whites and Africans (and to a lesser extent Indians and coloureds) has established a close correspondence between race and class, which makes the conflict much more intractable. But the communal conflict is essentially not a disguised class struggle. It is between two communities, predominantly Afrikaner and African respectively, whose primary aim is control of the State and possession of a historic homeland. Accordingly, virtually all political parties, trade unions and other public associations are communally based and emphasise the promotion of communal interests rather than purely class objectives.

Many analysts dispute this emphasis on a communal* struggle. They stress the pursuit by whites of material rewards and privileges, and consider nationalist convictions of lesser importance. The emphasis on material interests as the perceived purpose of the apartheid system also informs political forecasts. The unspoken assumption of many analysts is that

---

* I prefer communal to ethnic. Ethnic is too narrow a category for it refers to a group with a common belief in a shared ancestry and history. This would fit the Afrikaners, but not the larger white community, or, for that matter, the African or larger black community. Moreover, the ethnic style of politics is linked more particularly with the efforts to define group exclusively and to give vivid expression to its historic heritage and cultural symbols. Communalism, by contrast, operates within less rigid boundaries and is more geared to the politics of group entitlement which makes special claims upon the state for rewards and services on the basis of past performance (or exploitation). However, the emotional bond sustaining communalism and its implicit nationalist claims should not be underestimated. I use the terms communal and nationalist interchangeably, although Afrikaner nationalism in the past had a much stronger insistence on exclusive 'possession' of the land than the present-day communalism.

114

after a cost-benefit analysis of material prospects the more affluent and secure Afrikaners will settle for majority rule.[1]

No one would deny that the substantially greater rewards and privileges whites enjoy exercise a powerful influence upon the way in which whites (or blacks) think about the system and their political strategies. Yet historians are only too aware that people time and again have acted against what analysts at the time (or retrospectively) considered to be their greater material interests.[2] This is not due to a particular form of short-sightedness. If history teaches one thing it is that both ruling élites and subordinates attach at least as much weight to socio-political considerations such as communal or national status, identity and autonomy as to their evaluation of their immediate material interests.

To investigate the prospects of a possible settlement between the two contending nationalisms it is necessary to analyse briefly the burden of the past and the nature of the two nationalisms. Only then will we be able to assess the prospects of a resolution of the conflicting claims about national status and identity.

THE BURDEN OF A SETTLER SOCIETY

South African history is unique in the way in which post-1870 industrial society adapted to pre-industrial social relations and used a modernized state apparatus to intensify the forms of oppression established originally by the settler society. This was the real turning-point in South African history: Africans were incorporated into the industrial work-force without undermining white settler domination. This shifts the spotlight to the history of South Africa as a settler society, where the still powerful racial and national divisions originated. These divisions were mainly the horizontal racial divide between whites and blacks and the vertical one between Afrikaners and English-speakers.[3] The basic antagonisms between white and black flowed from slavery and frontier conquest. White settlers increasingly believed themselves to be bearers of a superior non-African system which had to be preserved against being swamped, against *gelykstelling*. The settlers' socio-political dominance enabled them to establish and perpetuate their position of privilege, in the process degrading slaves, serfs and their descendants. The status, security and ultimate survival of settler society was as vital a concern as reaping the material benefits of domination. As George Frederickson concludes: 'The degradation of non-whites frequently served to bind together the white population, or some segment of it, to become a way of life, and not simply a cover for economic exploitation.[4]

During the accelerated industrialization which occurred after the 1870s, the inter-dependence between whites and Africans increased but this did not dissolve the basic divide between the Afrikaner (and larger white) com-

115

munity and the Africans. In the course of the 20th century the political system became akin to one of 'nations' interacting within the same territory with highly crystallised, almost caste-like status differences between two formations.[5]

This, then, is the significance for contemporary South Africa of the failure of industrialization to alter the basic elements of settler domination and black exclusion. As Sam Nolutshungu cogently observes, the main political cleavages have continued to be ethnic, racial and national. As a result, the State is challenged by the subordinate population primarily in terms of their subordination as a nation rather than of exploitation. Accordingly, blacks issue their challenge primarily in the form of a nationalist movement rather than a class struggle. The State's attempt to gain widespread black acceptance through reform faces virtually insuperable obstacles. The reason is that the continuing national domination (which corresponds with the racial cleavage) undercuts the State's efforts to extend its base by incorporating the vulnerable black middle class and establishing the domination of middle-class people across colour lines.[6]

The National Party, as a 'poor settler' regime in South Africa, has to operate within the constraints imposed by its constituency – settlers' descendants. Like the Protestants in Northern Ireland or the Jews in Israel it is concerned with national status and prestige as well as material standing. Since it is ultimately political power which preserves 'colonial birthrights', any dilution of that power, even symbolic political co-optation of the 'natives', raises an outcry from sections that fear betrayal. The conflict in South Africa (like that in Northern Ireland or Israel) is not rooted in the religious or racial differences as such. It stems from challenges to the identity – which could be either racially or religiously defined – of the most prestigious community that emerged from the period of settler domination. In South Africa the need for political co-optation is greater, for unlike Northern Ireland, the country is ruled by a demographically shrinking minority. However, here too the historical forces continually undercut a party such as the Progressive Federal Party which proposes, in the name of enlightened self-interest, the political integration of the subordinates. They also influence the leadership of the governing party to believe that it cannot move much beyond a carefully controlled co-optation policy without encountering major resistance from the right wing.

Despite its fairly recent technocratic gloss the National Party is still mainly informed by the precepts of Afrikaner nationalism. The nature of this nationalism is discussed briefly below.

AFRIKANER NATIONALISM

The rise of Afrikaner nationalism is arguably the single most important political development of the first half of 20th-century South Africa. Yet the

116

nature of this nationalism, its sustaining power, and its potential for coming to terms with oppositional forces are still poorly understood.

What, indeed, are the chances of this nationalism dissolving itself or committing 'voluntary suicide'? Is there a prospect of national politics being replaced by class-based politics that can accommodate majority rule? To answer this, it is important to know whether nationalism is basically economistic in nature in the sense that material considerations are of overriding importance, or whether non-material or even 'irrational' influences (ideas and sentiments about national identity and status) have acquired a force of their own and play an important, even decisive, role.

Given the present South African government's obsession with ethnicity, almost as if – to use Neville Alexander's terms – it was an elegant variation of Divine Will, it must be stressed that there is no primordial force called ethnicity which makes groups cohere.[7] It is also not inevitable that competing nationalisms will emanate from a divided society undergoing rapid industrialization.[8] It is structural forces within a particular set of circumstances that will prompt a group to choose nationalism rather than, say, socialism as a political strategy.

The emergence of a nationalism, and the form it assumes, depends on a society's founding history, the population mix, the differential access groups have to power and education, and the nature of the economy. The fact that South Africa has never known a strong socialist movement transcending colour divisions has much to do with its settler origins. Unskilled Afrikaner workers entering the gold or diamond mines never forgot that they, like their fathers, commanded a position of authority and superiority over Africans in the pre-industrial period. That, together with the political power and better education they enjoyed, made them resist the rigid industrial discipline and abuse to which Africans were subjected.[9] It also made them reject industrial *gelykstelling*. Their attitude is well expressed in the words of DF Malan in the 1930s: 'The white man, because he is white, is expected – whatever his chances in the labour market – to maintain a white standard of living ... you can understand that in the circumstances, the competition for the white man is killing.'[10] The cheap wages that blacks for a variety of reasons had to accept, especially in the mining and agricultural sectors, made the development of common worker interests impossible.

Thus there were powerful reasons for a basic divergence of racial identity which has continued to manifest itself in the us–them syndrome. This was reinforced by the segregation policies of the 19th and 20th centuries. But this does not explain the particular form of nationalism that arose among Afrikaners. Theorists usually distinguish between (i) territorial nationalism, associated with Western Europe, where the thrust was to create out of the people living in a State a culturally homogeneous nation which governed itself, and (ii) ethnic nationalisms (or ethno-nationalisms), occurring in multi-ethnic States such as those of Eastern Europe. Here members of cul-

117

tural groups for various reasons develop a vivid sense of oneness of kind. Their identification with their ethnic group drives them to claim full political control in the name of ethnic self-determination. If successful, they set themselves up as *the* nation while relegating others to subordinate minorities. Unlike territorial nationalisms which have been built on a high culture (e.g. German or Italian), ethno-nationalisms usually have to embark on social engineering and ideological invention to create a high culture and establish a close linkage between State and culture.[11]

Afrikaner nationalism obviously fits the category of ethno-nationalism, but why did Afrikaners over time develop such a vivid sense of oneness of kind? The answer seems to lie in the great advantage ethno-nationalism enjoys as a form of political mobilisation. It combines a strategy to promote or defend the discrete interests of classes within the group with a dimension that relates to ethnic or communal power and status. The latter dimension is explicitly political and emotional. On occasion, outsiders even consider it irrational, to be dismissed with terms such as 'frontier' or 'laager' mentality rather than subject it to dispassionate analysis.

Recent analyses of Afrikaner nationalism concentrate on economistic explanations, and in some cases virtually exclude the political and emotional dimension.[12] There certainly was a profound economic dimension in the rise of Afrikaner nationalism. The fact that it first manifested itself during the first phases of industrialization is hardly coincidental. Industrial development is always uneven, leaving some groups behind or with a sense of relative deprivation. If inequalities are of an ethnic or cultural nature – as they were in the case of Afrikaners and English-speakers – groups with access to power and education often mobilise themselves under ethnic banners.

Industrialization also tends to generate ethno-nationalism for another reason. As Gellner has pointed out, industrialization requires workers to have shared generic skills. This in turn demands a standardised, homogeneous and centrally sustained high culture. In the South Africa of the late 19th century, English and Dutch functioned as high cultures. English would have established a monopoly had it not been for the Dutch/ Afrikaner intellectuals and 'clerks' (teachers, church ministers, attorneys, civil servants, etc.) who found their careers blocked by the English high culture. They became 'language manipulators':[13] people whose livelihood depended on the mastery of a language. It is they who turned an ethnic dialect into a modern language and then insisted that the State help elevate it to a high culture. They also made it their particular concern to minister to the sense of estrangement and exclusion which the uprooted urban Afrikaners experienced in the rough early phases of South African industrialization. It gave rise to a highly charged romantic nationalism which emphasised Afrikaner history and traditional values.[14]

It is also not difficult to give economic reasons why Afrikaner nationalism had such a sustaining power even after the 1940s when the early phase of industrialization had passed and most Afrikaners had become urbanised. The Nationalist government promised to promote a variety of interests – better producer prices and stricter labour controls for farmers, job reservation for workers, State contracts for businessmen, and an insistence on bilingualism for civil servants. Partly as a result of State aid, the Afrikaners experienced a dramatic economic advance between 1946 and 1977. By 1946, only a third of the Afrikaners could be considered middle class (being in white-collar urban jobs or reasonably secure farmers); by 1977 this had gone up to close to 70 per cent.[15]

But had nationalism merely been a disguised form of class politics, occurring particularly during early industrialization, one would expect it to have waned once the income gap between Afrikaners and English-speakers started to narrow, life-styles began to converge and the sharp polarisation of the early stages disappeared. And one would expect businessmen and workers across racial and ethnic divides to have been drawn towards a form of class-oriented politics. Had ethno-nationalism been masked class politics, there would indeed have been a chance of 'voluntary (ethnic) suicide' in order to promote class interests under different banners. However, if one looks at white politics over the past 20 years most trends point the other way. The PFP as the only party committed to integrative politics, never attracted more than 7 per cent of the Afrikaner vote, declining to 4 per cent in the 1987 election. White English-speakers have increasingly considered South Africa to be their homeland and a place where whites have considerable control over their political destiny. The support for the parties and candidates to the left of the NP and right-wing 'white homeland' parties declined from 30 per cent in 1977 to 27 per cent in 1981 to 18 per cent in 1987.

In literature there has been a strong tendency to present the NP and the government as the vehicle of the upper middle class and particularly of big business. However, the NP in fact has retained a fair spread in its class composition. In a 1986 poll, the party derived 20 per cent of its support from people in the 'upper middle' category of household income, 45 per cent from the 'middle' and 35 per cent from the 'lower-middle/lower' category. (The figures for the HNP/Conservative Party are 10, 49 and 41 per cent respectively.) In a crude fashion, these figures display the extent to which the National Party will have to square upper-middle class, middle and working-class interests. In recent extensive interviews with NP parliamentarians and ministers, Schlemmer found that the vast majority of these politicians were, above all, sensitive to the wishes of the party supporters. Most politicians wanted to effect a balance between the variety of interest groups within the Afrikaner national and the broader white community. None suggested that business interests and the large corporate sector had a particular influence on government.[16]

Ethno-nationalism, then, clearly cannot be explained in purely economistic terms. In his astute general observations of communal conflicts, Walker Connor remarks that statesmen and scholars (particularly Americans) err in assuming that economic considerations will be decisive in human affairs under conditions of communal strife. Connor concludes that economic factors 'are likely to come in a poor second when competing with the emotionalism of ethnic nationalism'.[17]

It was invariably emotive issues relating to national identity and status which triggered the major electoral shifts in South African political history. The Rebellion of 1914–15 (on the issue of South Africa's participation in World War I) paved the way for the NP's first breakthrough in the election of 1915 when it unexpectedly captured 27 seats. Fusion between Hertzog's NP and Smuts' South African Party, which was perceived as a threat to national sovereignty, led to the establishment of Malan's 'Purified' NP. This party may well have remained in the wilderness had South Africa's participation in the Second World War (seen as compromising South African autonomy) not destroyed the white middle ground. The NP won the 1948 election mainly on the basis of establishing Afrikaner control over their homeland.

Once in power, the NP government on several occasions made decisions which were 'irrational', judged purely on economic grounds. In the 1950s it barred many skilled immigrants from English-speaking countries who could have contributed greatly to economic growth. The government took the country out of the British Commonwealth in 1961, despite dire predictions about economic disaster, because it did not want to compromise national 'autonomy' and 'honour'. In 1986 the NP government deliberately invited sanctions and disinvestment (again disregarding dire predictions) in order to demonstrate its immunity from foreign pressure. Despite this, English-speaking support for the NP went up to over 50 per cent in the 1987 election, compared to below 30 per cent in 1981.

This suggests that the political and emotional dimension of the ethno-national strategy – issues relating to ethnic or communal power and status – is crucial, and indeed decisive. It is important to realise why this is so. In his study, Kedourie warns against dismissing nationalist ideology as hardly worthy of analysis. In fact, nationalist identity is the creation of a nationalist doctrine rather than the other way round.[18] Nationalism builds on the Kantian doctrine that self-determination is the supreme political good. This leads to the central nationalist claim that self-determination can only be realised through national self-determination in a world 'naturally' divided into nations.[19] This forms the basis for both Afrikaner nationalism, and its ideological instrument, apartheid. President PW Botha as leader of the moderate wing of Afrikaner nationalism has clearly internalised the doctrine of the 'group' or 'nation', making it the guiding principle of his approach to politics.[20]

The NP's insistence on self-determination is no longer cast in narrow Afrikaner terms, but rather has a broader white community orientation. It embraces a combination of elements such as a distinctive life-style, a sense of origin and identity, the psychological satisfaction of in-group community life (which includes schools), standards of public order, behaviour and respectability, and sufficient control over the allocation of resources and the maintenance of security to ensure the continuation of these benefits.[21]

National Party interviewees nowadays seldom mention threats to the Afrikaans language and its related culture as among the most pressing problems or salient issues.[22] However, this does not mean that Afrikaner ethnicity is no longer an issue. It is because the culture is so well protected within the dominant white community that it does not surface as a concern. This may change rapidly the moment political control is threatened, not to speak of a possible take-over by the ANC as vanguard of the African nationalists. As Gellner observed in a general context: 'The high (literate) culture in which they have been educated is, for most men, their most precious investment, the core of their identity, their insurance, and their security.'[23] Ultimately ethno-nationalism goes beyond culture, and involves a close emotional identification with the State, national institutions such as Parliament and the army, and national symbols and values. Much of the talk about a peaceful transfer of power in South Africa misses the fundamental point: that the Afrikaners and the larger white nation consider their sovereignty as precious. It is not something to be bartered away.

AFRICAN NATIONALISM

In a new study on nationalism, Benyamin Neuberger makes a useful distinction between approaches to nationalism on the African continent. There was (i) *the liberal-democratic approach to national self-determination*, which demands respect for basic human rights, protection of minorities, equality for all individuals and groups, free elections and the right to participate in government. It found best expression in French West Africa during the 1950s where the African élite was ready to transcend national self-determination for the sake of the full democratization of the French Empire.

There was also (ii) *the national approach to self-determination*. This was pursued under the banner of anti-colonial nationalism which aimed to restore, albeit in modified form, a golden age which had come to an abrupt end through foreign conquest. Neuberger declares: 'The national school of self-determination defines the achievement of independence as the goal of national self-determination. National self-determination is perceived as fulfilled as long as the citizens of the nation are ruled by their 'kith and kin'.[24] In the white-ruled Rhodesia and in South Africa, the crucial question was and is 'who are the people in the territory who constitute the appropriate self for self-determination?'[25]

The question, then, is how Africans in South Africa see the political self. In meetings such as the one in Dakar in July 1987 with a group of internal South Africans, the ANC leadership strongly emphasised its liberal-democratic credentials. This is based in the first place on the Freedom Charter, adopted in 1955, and the secession of some of the Africanists who established the Pan-Africanist Congress (PAC) in 1959. In fact, the Charter's use of the term 'national' is ambiguous. One of the key phrases reads, 'All national groups shall have equal rights', which, some of the Charter's critics claim, may suggest the creation of four nations – Africans, coloureds, Indians and whites.[26] Another clause states: 'The national wealth of our country, the heritage of all South Africans, shall be restored to the people.' Charter supporters argue that the word 'national' refers to all South Africans,[27] but the word 'restore' may suggest that it primarily has Africans in mind. And then, of course, there is the Charter's ringing opening phrase: 'South Africa belongs to all who live in it, black and white, and … no government can justly claim authority unless it is based on the will of the people.' This again suggests a liberal-democratic approach to self-determination.

The Charter is such a synthesized document that too much weight should not be attached to individual clauses. It reflects the three main strands which characterised the ANC during the 1950s, namely Charterist, workerist and Africanist. The Charterist position was aimed at constructing a broad-based movement transcending race and class to oppose apartheid. The workerist strand sought to build a political trade union movement that would 'harness workers' demands for economic amelioration to a political cause'.[28] It was to participate in the political struggle against pass laws, Bantu education and other forms of oppression.[29] The third strand was Africanism. This was for the first time openly expressed by the ANC's Programme of Action of 1949 and then again by the PAC. The PAC argued that the Programme of Action had proposed an ethnically assertive nationalism, which was diluted by the ANC alliance with the white-dominated Congress of Democrats and by the strategic influence of white communists within the ANC. In the PAC's view this influence expressed itself in the Charter's recognition of the rights and status of all national groups.

In the view of the Africanists an emphasis on 'multi-racialism' was dangerous because it would deprive the ANC of the most effective ideological means of inspiring a mass following and would perpetuate the African dependence on whites on which minority domination rested.[30] The PAC itself was ambiguous about the degree to which it wanted whites to be excluded. In his 1959 presidential address, Robert Sobukwe called for a government by the Africans for the Africans – and specified that 'everybody who owes his loyalty to Africa has to be regarded as African'. In a newspaper article, Sobukwe exhorted whites to adjust their outlook in such a fashion that 'Africa for the Africans ... could apply to them even though they are white'. Sobukwe, however, also stated that whites were for the present unable to pledge their loyalty to Africa, even if they were intellectual converts to the cause of African freedom, 'because they benefit materially from the present set-up', and so 'cannot completely identify themselves with that cause'.[31]

The crucial question is whether the ANC/PAC split concerns a fundamental disagreement over goals and ideology, or whether it is one on a lower level over discipline, strategy and tactics to promote nationalist goals.

The NP's shifts over the past ten years provided a classic case of a nationalist movement adapting its strategy, image and rhetoric without wishing to abandon its nationalist claims. No serious analyst has argued that the breakaway of Treurnicht's Conservatives in 1982 'proved' that the NP was less committed to Afrikaner rule or that it genuinely intended to share power with the coloured and Indian communities. In the case of the ANC, however, there is a surprising willingness to accept clauses in the Freedom Charter and the break with the PAC as sufficient proof that it was not in the first place committed to African nationalism but rather to an inclusive South African liberal democracy.

Like other nationalist movements, the ANC has above all been committed to building up an all-class front in its primary community, the Africans. Its goal is national self-determination in which the 'self' would undoubtedly be the Africans in the majority. Nelson Mandela spelled out the position in the Rivonia trial: 'The ideological creed of the ANC is, and always has been, the creed of African nationalism. It is not the concept of African nationalism expressed in the cry, "drive the white man into the sea". The African nationalism for which the ANC stands is the concept of freedom and fulfilment for the African people in their own land.'

The ANC's split with the PAC stemmed predominantly from struggles on leadership level on the Witwatersrand during the 1950s. At times, this threatened to destroy the movement. Bogged down by bannings, the Treason Trial and inexperienced or incompetent office-bearers, the Transvaal ANC was vulnerable to challenges. In a manner similar to the manoeuvres of Treurnicht's men during the two or three years prior to the 1982 NP/CP split, some Africanists exploited ideological differences in their struggle to gain control of the Transvaal ANC. Only when that failed did they break away, declaring, very much like Treurnicht in the case of Afrikaner nationalism, that they would form an organisation of their own to function as a 'custodian of traditional ANC policy'.[32] The PAC never succeeded in establishing followings in the Transvaal or the Eastern Cape, which either meant that there were no Africanists there – which is unlikely – or that they did not have any major ideological differences with the ANC.

The ANC enlistment of white support in the 1950s was a matter of strategy rather than principle. It realised that sympathetic whites were necessary to educate other whites on the evils of the pass system and to lead deputations to the government and local authorities. Apart from the communists, however, very few whites were integrated into the organisation and activities of the ANC. Jack Simons, an academic with a long association with the movement, states that while the ANC has had open membership since 1943, it made no considered attempt during its period of legitimacy to integrate non-Africans. After the movement had been driven into exile in the early 1960s, a substantial number of Indians, coloureds and whites were absorbed into the ANC. Nevertheless, until 1985 non-Africans were not included in the National Executive Committee of the ANC. Prior to the movement's Consultative Conference of that year, an ANC leader made a stand against non-African inclusion on the grounds that the ANC's struggle was first and foremost against white domination, and that Africans should liberate themselves under their own leadership. Commenting on this, Simons writes that there was 'an obvious contradiction between the approved policy of enlisting militants from all national groups and the proposed exclusion of non-Africans from the leadership'. He adds that 'an even more serious contradiction existed between this Africanist approach and the claims of Congress to represent all national groups in the struggle for a single South African nation'.[33] The conference of 1985 finally resolved the issue in favour of the participation of all South Africans in the work of the ANC on all levels.

In its ideology the same contradictions are evident. Two themes dating back to the late 1920s vie with each other. On the one hand the ANC proposes a non-racial struggle of all the classes (with the workers as a leading force), while on the other hand it calls for an Africanist struggle against white colonisation. Until very recently the latter theme dominated. The ANC slogan *Mayibuye i Afrika* is a demand for a return of the land of Africa to its indigenous inhabitants. There is little ambivalence on the issue of the appropriate self for self-determination. In a 1982 discussion of the two basic ANC documents, the Freedom Charter and the ANC's 'Strategy, Tactics and Programme', *Sechaba* states clearly: 'Our notion of the people identifies the African people as the main revolutionary force and the African people as a decisive component in it.'[34] The mainspring of the struggle was the mobilisation of the African people as a dispossessed and racially oppressed nation. In certain instances the ANC's actions deliberately coincide with Afrikaner nationalist events. In response to the Afrikaners' celebration of 16 December as the day symbolising their victory over the Africans, the ANC formed its military wing *Umkhonto we Sizwe* on the same date in 1961 and still celebrates it as the historic 'turning point in the long march to freedom'.[35]

The degree to which the ANC as a nationalist movement has an inclusive approach to its membership (as opposed to the PAC's exclusion of whites) is due more to strategic considerations imposed by its existence in exile, than any unified ideological commitment. In an analysis published in 1962, Feit wrote that the ANC had at all times sought to include all shades of African opinion. It was struggles over leadership, not ideology, which led to expulsions and splits. The disunity of the movement was so great that Nelson Mandela felt that should the ANC ever achieve its aims it would probably split into a number of political parties.[36] Exile, in contrast, enforced discipline, and also strengthened its commitment to an inclusive nationalism and non-racialism. Some African countries disliked the ANC's inclusion of whites as members but the movement's main concern was winning Western diplomatic recognition and support. In this struggle it made much more sense to grant South African whites a place in the sun than to acquire an image similar to that of the PAC, which sometimes appeared as if it wanted to drive the whites into the sea.

As a nationalist movement in exile, the ANC has had few problems with incorporating other organisations in its broad front despite ideological differences. Thus the leadership could laud the black consciousness movement for its organisational achievements and absorb part of the movement despite, as Oliver Tambo delicately phrased it, its 'limitations in seeing our struggle as racial'.[37] It was also able to welcome the establishment of the United Democratic Front, a movement with a great many non-African members. On the other hand, however, the ANC displays a typical nationalist suspicion of working-class mobilisation that may over time pose a challenge to the leadership. This probably accounts for the expulsion in the late 1970s of a group of workerists who felt that the ANC had failed in not having built the movement on the working class. These suspicions are also reflected in the ANC advice to the 1987 Cosatu national conference against adopting socialism as Cosatu policy.[38]

Building up a broad front of allies, does not mean that the ANC is no longer a nationalist movement at its core. Yet a broad front almost inevitably affects ideology. The ANC no longer uses the terms 'non-racial struggle of all classes' primarily in a Marxist sense but rather as liberals would in a stand against apartheid's enforced group membership. The degree to which this dimension can be strengthened will determine whether the ANC will be prepared to enter the arena of multi-party competition. For the moment, however, the nationalist temptation to assert hegemonic control over all oppositional forces remains very strong.

What route to nation-building the ANC and its allies will follow if they win power also depends on the values forged during the struggle for their liberation. The fight against apartheid rules out the building of a nation on the basis of distinct ethnic groups. Except in its earlier stages, the ANC never favoured the Afrikaners' brand of ethno-nationalism. Instead, the ANC insists on the forced unification of ethnic groups in a homogeneous nation. Like mass parties elsewhere on the African continent it envisages this nation-building project occurring under the direction of a highly centralised government. However, if the ANC in the course of its struggle is compelled to forge alliances and make political compromises, the Jacobin tendencies within this nationalism may be softened. A form of political and cultural pluralism could take root which may yield a form of nationalism that is *sui generis* on the continent.

DISPUTED TERRITORIES AND COMMUNAL CLAIMS

In South Africa the divisions between whites and blacks, and between Afrikaner and African nationalism remain deep and strongly felt. Recent times have witnessed a slight but not insignificant blurring of the divisions. The political barriers between Afrikaners and English-speaking whites have largely disappeared and the Government is increasingly drawing blacks into the administration and defence of the State. On the ANC side some strides have been made in the past years to redefine its struggle ideologically in non-racial, rather than nationalist, terms. However, this does not mean that the essence of either the NP or ANC has changed. On occasion their core thinking is revealed, for example when Chris Heunis states that 'it is in the long-term interest that the Afrikaner should always have the privilege of the leadership role'.[39] The ANC, on the other hand, while stressing that it is not exclusivist, insists that its primary task is the 'national liberation of the largest and most oppressed group – the African people'.[40] In a statement by the National Executive Committee in December 1986 the struggle is seen primarily in terms of the continuity of African resistance from the battle of Isandhlwana in 1879, through the Bambatha Uprising in 1906, up to the present time.

There does not appear to be much evidence that the disintegration of communal lines by class interests will occur. In the first place comparative studies show that ethnic and communal antagonisms are exacerbated by rapid urbanisation – and millions of Africans will become urbanised during the next two decades. Whites will attempt against considerable odds to preserve the life-styles to which they are accustomed. Blacks will challenge the headstart whites continue to enjoy by virtue of their access to virtually all the resources of the State – economic, educational, political, administrative and social. Expanded black education seems to be strengthening the black demand for equality in State services rather than weakening them. The tensions will greatly intensify once whites sense that the State may fall and the 'homeland' may be lost. Once the conflict reaches this stage it may well become non-negotiable. Then the struggle truly will be one of survival, involving the basic issue of personal and communal identity and integrity. It is not a question of the dominant group being massacred or driven into the sea, of which there is virtually no chance in South Africa. It is rather a question of dominant groups in deeply divided societies identifying so strongly with the ethnic homeland and State that they become part of their extended self. To lose control over the homeland 'is to risk the fragmentation of the self, an eventuality which people will resist with their very lives'.[41] Not much store should be put on rationality when dominant groups are driven to the wall. In a comparative study on Lebanon and South Africa, Theodor Hanf remarks: '(It) is by no means certain that economic considerations would govern the behaviour of a dominant group if it felt that its existence was threatened. A scorched-earth policy is hardly an economically rational concept. Nevertheless it is one often, and particularly, practised in civil wars between ethnic and religious groups.'[42]

CONCLUSION

Robert McNamara has summed up well the 'magic' political formula for peace in South Africa, also quoted in chapter 14 of this volume. It must, he declared, assure blacks of full participation in genuine political power. And it must protect whites against a winner-takes-all form of majority rule. At the moment the NP government is insisting on considerably more. The *least* the government would settle for – after well-directed pressure and incentives – is co-equality or a form of dualism. On the one hand one would have a white-led political group stressing group rights and choosing their own representatives. On the other hand one would have a political bloc headed by African nationalists stressing individual rights and representation. A system built on freedom of association, i.e. with each person having the freedom to decide which bloc to support, would constitute a decisive break with apartheid. Once there is mutual acceptance, these two blocs will be able to negotiate a system in which they would have parity of representation on legislative and executive levels, and with a chief executive appointed on a rotating basis. The challenge would be to build a new nation over time which would transcend both Afrikaner and African nationalism.

Such a system is far less than what blacks are struggling for, but also much more than they currently enjoy. It may be the only realistic intermediate goal for those wanting *peaceful* change in South Africa. Only a government with a clearly representative black and white component will have the moral authority to use force and to meet the security and identity needs of both whites and blacks.

To arrive at a compromise, a strategy of gradualism is necessary to de-escalate tensions. Useful insights can be gleaned from the studies advocating de-escalation in the USA-Russian conflict: Etzioni's *The hard way to peace* and Osgood's *An alternative to war and surrender*. The central principle in this approach is a series of unilateral actions that induced – or at least provided – an opportunity for the adversary to reciprocate. Above all, it needs an attitude shift with respect to the realistic possibilities of change. Whites and blacks have no option but to find a way of living with one another that meets the crucial need for identity, dignity and security of all.

127

The alternative is Afrikaner and African nationalism becoming locked into a struggle to the bitter end over national identity and sovereignty.

NOTES

1 See for instance the perspective of an influential scholar: Heribert Adam, *Modernizing racial domination*, Los Angeles: California University Press, 1971, p 53; Heribert Adam and Hermann Giliomee, *Ethnic power mobilised: Can South Africa change?* New Haven: Yale University Press, 1979, pp 3–4, 301–302; Heribert Adam and Kogila Moodley, *South Africa without apartheid: Dismantling racial domination*, Berkeley: University of California Press, 1986, p 262.

2 See Barbara Tuchman, *The march of folly: From Troy to Vietnam*, New York: Ballantine Books, 1984.

3 For analyses of the development of stratification in the pre-industrial period see Robert Ross (ed.) *Racism and colonialism: Essays in ideology and social structure*, The Hague, 1982; and Richard Elphick and Hermann Giliomee (eds) *The shaping of South African society*, Cape Town: Longman, 1979, ch X.

4 George Frederickson, *White supremacy: A comparative study in American and South African history*, New York: Oxford UP, '98', pp 42–43.

5 Lawrence Schlemmer, 'South Africa's National Party government' in Peter Berger and Bobby Godsell, *A future South Africa*, Cape Town: Human and Rousseau, 1980, pp 40–44.

6 Sam Nolutshugu, *Changing South Africa*, Manchester: Manchester University Press, 1982, pp 147–150, 204–207.

7 For an excellent discussion of this in the Northern Ireland context, see Michael MacDonald's *Children of wrath*, Cambridge: Cambridge University Press, 1986, particularly pp 147–148. Also relevant is a recent comparative study of the decisive role of settlers in Algeria and Ireland in wrecking integrative policies which aim to extend political participation rights to wider native strata. See Ian Lustick's *State building failure in British Ireland and French Algeria*, Berkeley: Institute of International Studies, 1985.

8 Neville Alexander, *Sow the wind*, Johannesburg: Skotaville, 1985, pp 126–153. There is an interesting debate about the emergence of nationalism between Ernest Gellner, *Nations and nationalism*, Oxford: Basil Blackwell, 1983, who insists on a connection with early industrialization as something of a sociological law, and Elie Kedourie, who in *Nationalism* (London: Hutchinson, 1985) emphasises the force of ideas and gives examples of nationalism occurring outside the context of early industrialization.

9 Rob Turrell, 'Kimberley: Labour and compounds, 1871–1882', in Shula Marks and Richard Rathbone (eds), *Industrialisation and Social change in South Africa: African class formation, culture and consciousness, 1870–1930*, London: Longman, 1982, pp 45–76.

10 Cited by J Lever, 'White strategies in a divided society: The development of South African labour policy' unpublished paper.

11 This paragraph draws on Anthony Smith's *The ethnic revival*, Cambridge: Cambridge UP, 1981, pp 18–19; Gellner, *Nations and nationalism*, pp 97–101; Kedourie, *Nationalism*, pp 131–133.

12 A case in point is Dan O'Meara, *Volkskapitalisme: Class, capital and ideology in the development of Afrikaner nationalism, 1934–1948*, Cambridge: Cambridge UP, 1983. For a more sophisticated social history approach see the volume edited by Shula Marks and Stanley Trapido, *The Politics of race, class and nationalism in twentieth century South Africa*, London: Longman, 1986.

13 The term is that of Hugh Seton-Watson, *Times Higher Educational Supplement*, 27 August 1982, pp 12–13.

14 I deal in greater detail with the origins of Afrikaner nationalism in two articles, one published in *South African Historical Journal* 17 (1987) and the other in *Journal of Southern African Studies*, Vol 14, No 1 (1987).

15 I discuss this more fully in Adam and Giliomee, *Ethnic power mobilised*, pp 145–176.

16 Schlemmer *et al*, 'South Africa's National Party government'; pp 19–28.

17 Walker Connor, 'Nation-building or Nation-destroying', *World politics*, (1972) 24, p 343.

18 Kedourie, *Nationalism*, p 146.

19 Kedourie, *Nationalism*, pp 9–27.

20 Koos van Wyk and Deon Geldenhuys, *Die Groepsgebod in PW Botha se politieke oortuigings*, Johannesburg: RAU, 1987.

21 Schlemmer, 'South Africa's NP government', p 27.

22 Schlemmer, 'South Africa's NP government', p 24.

23 Gellner, *Nations and nationalism*, p 111.

24 Benyamin Neuberger, *National self-determination in post-colonial Africa*, Boulder: Lynne Rienner, 1986, pp 12–13.

25 Neuberger, *National self-determination*, p 41.

26 No Sizwe, *One Azania, one nation*, London: Zed Press, 1979.

27 Raymond Suttner and Jeremy Cronin, *30 Years of the Freedom Charter*, Johannesburg: Ravan, 1985, p 136.

28 E Feit, *Workers without weapons*, Hamden, 1975.

29 Paul Maylam, *A history of the African people of South Africa*, London: Croom Helm, 1986, pp 188–189.

30 Tom Lodge, *Black politics in South Africa since 1945*, Johannesburg: Ravan Press, 1983, pp 82–86.

31 Lodge, *Black politics*, pp 84–85.

32 Peter Raboroko, 'The Africanist Case', *Africa South*, April–June 1960.

33 Jack Simons, 'The Freedom Charter: Equal rights and freedoms' in *The Freedom Charter: A commemorative publication*, London, 1985, pp 102–166.

34 Cited in *The Freedom Charter*, pp 75–76.

35 ANC pamphlet, 'Born of the people', Statement by O R Tambo, 16 December 1986.

36 Edward Feit, *South Africa: The dynamics of the African National Congress*, London: Oxford UP, 1962, pp 11–12.

37 Documents of the Second National Consultative Conference of the ANC, Zambia, 16–23 June 1985, p 13.

38 *Financial Mail*, 24 July 1987, 'Political game plan'.

39 I expand on this in an article 'The Botha quest: sharing power without losing control.' *Leadership SA*, 2.2, 1983, pp 27–35 and in 'Apartheid, verligtheid and liberalism', in Jeffrey Butier, Richard Elphick and David Welsh (eds), *Democratic liberalism in South Africa*, Middletown: Wesleyan Press, 1986, pp 363–383.

40 See the critical comments of Robert Fatton 'The African National Congress of South Africa: The limitations of a revolutionary strategy', *Canadian Journal of African Studies*, pp 593–608.

41 These comments apply to a future South Africa although they were made in the Israeli context: Group for Advancement of Psychiatry, *Self-involvement in the Middle East*, New York, 1978, pp 489–503.

42 Theodor Hanf, 'Lessons which are never learnt: minority rule in comparative prospective', in Heribert Adam (ed), *The limits of reform politics*, Leiden: E.J. Brill, 1983, p 27.

13

AN OVERVIEW OF PAPERS AND DISCUSSIONS CONTRIBUTED DURING THE SYMPOSIUM

The Editors

In a situation as complex as that of South Africa and on a topic as wide-ranging as that of negotiation one can scarcely hope for tight coherence and a sharpness of focus in academic and political debate. As was expected, the papers and the discussions on the topic of political resolution at the symposium touched on myriad themes.

The debate was lively and some very valuable suggestions and observations were made on the topic at hand. (See chapter 14 for the major suggestions as regards routes to resolution.) Many important questions were raised and problems identified during the discussions. Since the first step in any intelligent analysis is to highlight the important problems, these issues serve as an excellent introduction to the final assessment.

In this chapter an attempt is made at capturing the major content of all the preceding chapters and discussions, by repeating the fundamental questions and the major dilemmas; all in our view very relevant to a serious search for solutions to the current impasse. These themes are presented as briefly as possible, our main intention being to identify 'building blocks' and 'stumbling-blocks' as regards the construction of possible routes towards a resolution.

MAJOR POINTS FROM THE PAPERS

Deputy Minister van der Merwe gives a clear outline of the government position on negotiations. The outline confirms the fact that the framework imposes some strict constraints. While it can be interpreted generously as a model which could allow blacks as much power as whites in a future dispensation, certain non-negotiables are clearly signalled. Whites will not lose the power base of a racially demarcated system of voting and the use of violence or disruption as methods of increasing leverage during negotiation will not be tolerated as long as the government enjoys its present position of legal and administrative control.

However, a concession is made to social-democratic goals in Deputy

Minister van der Merwe's statement that 'full' capitalism in the classic sense is not appropriate for South Africa. It is also clear that the government accepts the need to broaden the base of legitimacy by negotiating with as full a spectrum of leaders as possible, barring those who are associated with violent strategies.

It is not clear whether or not the latter constraint would exclude all members of the ANC. Recent statements about Nelson Mandela by Dr van der Merwe in his new capacity as Minister suggest that the issue of violence may have become more complex. We consider that provided intentions are signalled which the government would interpret as constructive, an association with the military strategy of the ANC (as opposed to direct involvement) may not be conclusive grounds for exclusion from negotiation.

What is also clear from Dr van der Merwe's outline is that the government is not so desperately anxious to negotiate with all legitimate leaders as to renege on its principles for negotiation. The framework for negotiation suggests that an offer is made from a desire to negotiate rather than from an overriding need to resolve a pressing crisis.

Dr Steenkamp's contribution is refreshing in that it is brutally frank on certain issues where other government spokesmen frequently adopt euphemisms. Steenkamp unabashedly defends a formal racial basis of participation. His grounds for rejecting the KwaZulu-Natal Indaba proposals make it clear that there is a strong group in government which requires cast-iron guarantees of white power in a future dispensation; guarantees that whites will be classified to vote as whites.

Steenkamp also emphasises another major impediment to a negotiated resolution in South Africa: the enormous costs of the rapid equalisation of services and social infrastructure for all South Africans which a negotiated resolution would require. Some limitations on the rights to equal fiscal benefits are deemed necessary in a(n) (extended) phase of transition. This obviously implies a corresponding limitation on the power of majority representatives, and as such places a serious damper on the prospects of success of negotiations.

Johan Steenkamp raises a vital issue in quoting Chief Buthelezi to the effect that no group should dictate to any other group how it should express its self-determination. This is in a sense reassuring to white Nationalists but at the same time calls into question a *general* principle of race classification, applicable to all people in South Africa.

Jannie Gagiano's case-study on Stellenbosch student attitudes is a useful caution to those observers who might conclude that the coherence of the ruling group is rapidly eroding and that conciliatory views will be impressed on the white political leadership by emerging sub-élites.

Gagiano points out that such a perception may be erroneously based on using support for the National Party as a criterion. Beyond this there is what he terms 'regime support' which implies endorsement of the goals of the political establishment without necessarily implying specific support for the National Party. He shows that among Stellenbosch students, who might be expected to be in the vanguard of defections from regime support among Afrikaners, there is no more than a 10 to 15 per cent minority outside the framework of regime values and objectives.

Turning to the extra-parliamentary forces, Paulus Zulu provides us with a convincing, indeed moving, account of the existential anguish under apartheid which has goaded the black youth into spear-heading internal resistance in South Africa. He quite eloquently reveals how a sense of hopelessness and of 'nowhere to go' has fed a surging idealism which has little concern for the 'nuts and bolts' of economics or administration. He reminds us of the 'millennial vision' which motivates youth protestors and the conviction that if a system is to be acceptable it has to be the *opposite* of any system currently ensconced.

This idealism, plus a certain stoicism which has emerged from the fire of township violence, while understandable, holds no hope for attitudes of compromise and conciliation on the part of the very groupings which have precipitated the crisis of legitimacy in South Africa. If the youth which Zulu describes are to endorse or judge the outcomes of negotiation, they are hardly likely to be more conciliatory than fearful and self-concerned whites. Indeed, the two sets of sentiments seem capable of reinforcing each other indefinitely.

Van Zyl Slabbert's contribution is brief and to the point, and also lucid in outlining the gulf of political assumptions which separate the major agencies which would have to participate in negotiations. He contrasts the 'total' strategies of the government and those of the ANC more clearly than was done before. Slabbert's sympathies lie with the resistance movements but as one of the country's most competent analysts he warns them against attempts to challenge the State at the centre. He makes the useful point that the South African conflict is not like a civil rights struggle with the hopeful assumption that injustices will be corrected. It is a struggle for power and therefore much more akin to the conflict societies of Eastern Europe than to struggles for rights in the West. He anticipates that decentralised challenges, or conflicts in functional areas such as education are much more likely to bring gains, however marginal, than head-on confrontations over central State power.

Mark Swilling is in a sense more hopeful. He too focuses attention on the possibilities of local negotiations. He points out that, inflamed rhetoric notwithstanding, there were leaders in the internal resistance who were realistic and prepared to negotiate. He claims that despite having been removed through detentions and arrests, these middle-level leaders still have massive followings and could, if allowed to mobilise again, turn out to be actors of great strategic importance in the resolution of conflict at community level. Although he dismisses the unrealistically confrontational stances taken by township activists too lightly, he makes the seemingly valid point that at the initial stages their actions were grievance based, and should their signal role be accepted in negotiations for the removal of those grievances, they could counter-balance more radical forces which have been stimulated by security action.

Jenkins displays impatience with popular views of the crisis in South Africa. The 'nuclear reactor' of South African society, 'never goes critical'. A 'wobbly equilibrium' could persist for many years yet. He appeals to analysts to jettison the distorted perceptions of imminent disaster in favour of 'respectful analysis' which takes full account of the resilience of State power.

Theo Hanf provides some concrete international and historical verification of Jenkins' warnings. He reviews some 32 cases of communal conflict and concludes that one-quarter have yielded nothing but protracted and bitter endemic violence, that negotiated resolutions have been achieved in less than half the cases and that in 50 per cent of these, there was a mutual recognition that coexistence was impossible, resulting in partition. Worst of all he points out that most cases of coexistence through compromise were preceded by bloody struggles.

He also points out that although privilege and material inequality are keynote features in South Africa, group consciousness is not rooted solely in power and privilege. Furthermore, as in the case of Poland, for example, the conditions for negotiation simply do not exist in South Africa. He observes that 'what has proved to be the optimal mobilising ideology for each side … proves utterly unsuitable as an instrument to persuade the other side'. White communalism or a bicommunal resolution could only be viable if the black majority were to endorse it – a most unlikely development. Majoritarianism, particularly if accompanied by socialist 'Jacobinism' is completely inappropriate for minority interests.

He draws attention to the tragedy and unsuitability of the clear and simple ideologies and believes that it is important to begin to think about diluted, complex, 'syncretistic' ideologies which could reduce the sharpness of the conflicts. As we shall indicate later, however, the political obsession on all sides with the great rewards of wielding central State power make meaningful dilution most unappealing to the actors involved.

Hanf makes a very important point, however, when he says that negotiation in advance of widespread violence is unlikely unless or 'until the definition of the framework and the respective objectives of negotiation become less incompatible'. He recommends a shift from racial thinking on both sides to an acceptance of *culture* as a way of bringing the parties closer together. In general, however, the need to strive towards making objectives less incompatible is cardinal. This will be a major topic of the final chapter.

As editors we shall not review our own contributions since major elements thereof will reappear in the final chapter. We subsequently turn to the discussions at the symposium.

DISCUSSIONS AT THE SYMPOSIUM

The issue of time

It is increasingly realised that serious negotiation for a settlement in South Africa could not commence soon. Although Van Zyl Slabbert warned participants in the symposium that the political situation was unpredictable and that negotiations could take everyone by surprise, the general view was that the situation was either in a pre-negotiation phase, when conditions for negotiation could be established, or in the very early stages of a build-up to a settlement. One government official argued that all the relevant formations, both in the government and extra-parliamentary camps, were in the process of consolidation and of defining positions and strategies, and that little overt action could be expected.

This recognition, however, was far from conforting for a cross-section of South African academics and political actors. The sense of urgency was pervasive and a number of participants issued the customary warnings that time was running out for a solution, or that precious time was being lost. Participants from abroad, with wider comparative experience of societies in conflict, were more philosophical. Simon Jenkins, although obviously endorsing the desirability of a settlement, as well as the necessity for addressing problems of breaches in the rule of law, again posed what was for South Africans the awkward question of whether or not it was at all realistic to expect a 'solution' in the foreseeable future. Many governments were able to manage problems of political illegitimacy for extended periods. 'Equilibrium' did not necessarily require desirable solutions, and an equilibrium in the conflict was a not implausible outcome for South Africa. The paper by Theo Hanf (chapter 11) also presents this uncomfortable reality. Jenkins ascribed the sense of urgency in part to the rise of sociological models in the analysis of the South African situation. The short historical purview of sociology robbed the observer of the time-depth of historical analyses, in the context of which societal 'crises' of legitimacy could persist for decades or centuries.

This historical perspective notwithstanding, the South African issue will continue to evoke a sense of urgency, and this was also true of the discussions at the symposium. Having acknowledged that a resolution was not in the immediate offing, participants turned to the issue of how best to facilitate developments towards it.

Process versus content

There was considerable discussion on the importance or relevance, at this early stage, of end-goals or models of resolution. An analogy of purchasing a motor car was used. The prospective buyer need not specify the model in advance but might identify particular specifications and characteristics, leaving the make and model to emerge later. Indeed, the point was made that too early a promotion of particular end-goals could inhibit the process.

With some exceptions which will be addressed later, this viewpoint was generally favoured, and participants explored aspects of the process of development towards negotiations. The following arguments emerged:

Some government officials suggested that both sides should set out *short-term* targets, thereby hopefully providing a basis for discovering some elements common to all sides in the conflict.

In a sense the government has done this recently with the proposals for an interim National Council which could preside over negotiations on a future constitution, within which joint decision-making or consultation between representatives of all groups could take place on an interim basis. Swilling suggested that the ANC had also stated interim requirements such as the confinement of security forces to barracks, the release of political prisoners and the repeal of repressive laws. Quite clearly the contexts signalled thus far within which negotiation could take place still leave the protagonists very far apart.

Another interim initiative explored was that of small-scale negotiations around a particular issue (a rent-boycott) or at a level below that of the central issue of power (negotiations at the local, city or regional level).

Swilling emphasised again the process whereby black communities had become mobilised and despite violent confrontations with the State in the past, had been geared towards such negotiations until security action swept away the guiding leadership. Member of Parliament Dr Steenkamp made it clear, however, that even at a local level the content of such negotiations would be tested by government in terms of its overall constitutional framework (this being one major reason why the KwaZulu-Natal Indaba was rejected as outlined in chapter 5). Similarly, participants who had been at the meeting with the ANC in Dakar in 1987 stated that the ANC would also probably assess local-level negotiations against its plans for the eventual exercise of power at the centre.

There appeared to be scant chance that issue-related or local-level negotiations could occur or that progress would not be influenced by central power agendas. They could not steal a march on the broader political process.

While tensions between local-level negotiations and national political agendas should be assumed, most participants nonetheless felt that such 'piecemeal' initiatives were an essential part of an interim process. Some participants, mainly but not exclusively on the side of government, considered that the Regional Services Councils could form a framework for negotiation. At the same time all participants acknowledged that local black politics was in disarray and that a reconstruction of either municipal politics or community organisation in black areas was necessary as a first step.

Violence as an impediment?

This issue was extensively debated, as one might expect. Government speakers indicated that it was impossible to make a distinction between the political programme of the ANC and its armed struggle, the latter calling into question the sincerity of any signals that the organisation might send as regards potential flexibility.

Some of the other participants, while deploring violence, insisted that there was some equivalence between the ANC's armed struggle and government action in the form of coercive security measures. The question was raised as to whether or not the government has the sole right to exercise force and for what ends? Mention was made of viewpoints, such as that of Frank Chikane of the SA Council of Churches, that the moral conditions for a 'just war' against the State had been established, and the fact that extra-parliamentary movements questioned, on the basis of principles such as those of the Geneva Convention, the right of the government to exercise State authority, in view of its lack of legitimacy. Van Zyl Slabbert made the useful distinction between legality and legitimacy; the government was legal and therefore would continue to exercise its authority despite manifest lack of legitimacy. Apart from this consideration it was clear that the government had committed itself to a public position on the ANC's use of violence and could not be seen to be deviating significantly from this position.

Simon Jenkins once again introduced a sobering perspective. Arguing that one well-established international view was that violence could be seen as an extension of negotiation, he felt that South Africans had become fixated on the issue of both the security methods of the government and the violence of the ANC. Negotiations and the use of force could occur simultaneously and eventually would probably do so in South Africa. Indeed, if mutual coercion produced a stalemate then it could even facilitate discussion and negotiation. The task was to attempt to reduce the level and costs of violence while seeing it in the correct perspective.

Alf Stadler pointed out that most democracies had been born in violence. Paulus Zulu argued that the violence of internal resistance movements was a reaction to government impediments to the expression of protest. Mark Swilling referred to the ANC's Arusha Declaration that its violence was simply intended to bring about the conditions for political change. Various participants pointed out that since the government had effective control of most levers of administration and social control, violence and destabilisation was an inevitable way in which the ANC would attempt to establish some power-equivalence. A balance of power was an essential precondition to negotiation.

While it appeared that many participants did not regard the issue of violence necessarily as an impediment to negotiation, a few were very mindful of some very dangerous implications of violence. Basing his argument on results obtained from his comparative studies, Theo Hanf reminded the symposium that programmed violence could move beyond itself, producing a situation of 'armed anomie'. The ANC could lose control of violence, warlords could enter the fray, militant youths could develop their own fragmented agendas and a host of particular or personal factors could turn the strategy into self-perpetuating destabilisation of the programmes of both protagonists.

Thus while violence, theoretically, could be seen as a possible adjunct to negotiations there are nevertheless dangers and difficulties. Perhaps the greatest difficulty is that the government is a viable legal agency, majority-based political illegitimacy notwithstanding, and it would be well-nigh impossible to expect it to willingly allow internal social control to fragment. The tragic implication of violence on the part of the resistance movements is that it would have to escalate dramatically, at great cost, before it could force the government to negotiate.

Signalling of constructive intentions

Whatever the implications of violence in a general sense, Mark Swilling strongly emphasised the fact that numerous local resistance movements, after having gone through an escalating cycle of protest and coercive strategies such as consumer boycotts, had achieved a point where they had been willing to negotiate about local grievances and issues of concern in the townships. At the local level a 'balance' of mutual costs had emerged and local chambers of commerce and other white establishment formations had been engaged in discussions. At this point, he claimed, the security agencies had swept in and detained the local community leadership, effectively decapitating the negotiation initiatives, as in the case of the National Education Crisis Committee and various local initiatives in the Eastern Cape and Natal.

This raised the problem of how constructive intentions could be 'signalled' and whether or not the government would be receptive to such signals. Overarching quasi-revolutionary rhetoric of resistance movements at national level made the deciphering of signals extremely difficult. The lack of past alliances between township groupings and establishment agencies which could mediate and signal intentions well in advance was another problem. The unwillingness of township formations to interact with the established local institutions of government (local town councils) was a further problem, since government would not willingly see the status of its own agencies usurped.

Clearly this was in area of great complexity with numerous very delicate issues involved. It was of such importance, however, that participants all agreed that a further symposium should be convened specifically on this issue (which has subsequently occurred).

The issue of trust

In a deeply polarised society and particularly one in which there has been systematic discrimination against one group and where the conflict has taken the form of mobilisation for violent confrontation, and counter-mobilisation of sentiment (i.e. mutual vilification or even demonisation), lack of mutual trust is without doubt a severe impediment to negotiation. In some instances this need not preclude negotiation, as already discussed, but in these cases a balance of power or of coercive force usually creates an artificial trust in the process. Both sides can depend on the other to adhere to the terms of negotiation simply because it may be more costly not to do so.

However, in the case of the South African government and the resistance movements (particularly the ANC), this condition does not hold. Although both have coercive potential and can inflict damage on the other, the power which is wielded is of a different order. The ANC has no more than potentially serious power to disrupt whereas the government has overwhelming power to impose its administrative system and to maintain this organisational coherence.

This particular pattern implies that trust in the negotiation process has to be created in a less than fortuitous environment. This can only be done if both sides consistently and honestly communicate their intentions over a period long enough to begin to modify mutually unattractive images. What intentions are the sides willing to communicate and how believable are they?

The stance of government on this vital issue has been spelt out on numerous occasions but was repeated during the workshop by Deputy Minister Stoffel van der Merwe, and Dr Johan Steenkamp, the National Party Member of Parliament. Their views and various government statements indicate that the government did not wish to impose limitations in regard to negotiations. It would not table blueprints and it was prepared to negotiate on an open agenda. However, the government position, which it would obviously argue for in any negotiations, was that of equal power-sharing within a system allowing for the 'self-determination' of whites, implying the maintenance of some form of group basis for participation.

Kobus Jordaan, a senior official in the Department of Constitutional Development Services, teased out some of the complexities from within the larger context and identified some of the difficulties. Because the government position is so vital his contribution is presented at some length:

Presently, elements in black communities suggest that they are under the impression that the government is not serious in its commitment to share power with blacks. They are not sure of the government's intentions, and many think that the government is just trying to reform apartheid. This distrust will have to be broken down ... To allay white fears and to reassure the blacks that the government is serious about power-sharing it will have to spell out its intentions more clearly in an open debate and at the same time obtain absolute clarity in the inner circle regarding its bottom lines without putting these on the table as 'pre-conditions'. Government will have to be more open regarding its vision of a future South Africa ... One can say that equal power-sharing does not mean the same thing to all (white) nationalists. Can there one day be a black president? Apparently the President says no, Mr Pik Botha yes – this must be confusing the black people. It must be very difficult for National Party MPs to have to spell out what is really meant by power-sharing ...

I am further convinced that if there had been greater clarity on the government's intentions on power-sharing and if the National Party had participated as a full member in the Indaba, the Indaba would not have forced through the present proposals. As a matter of fact, we were told that much by key persons within the Indaba.

I reiterate that I believe that it is imperative for the government to spell out more clearly its intentions regarding the 'how' of power-sharing. Once it does this the negotiating process will be facilitated greatly because then black groupings will have little choice but to accept the government's commitment. The proof of the pudding will then lie in participation.

Blacks, on the other hand, will have to scale down their preconditions. They will have to accept that the government is sincere in its commitment to share power. Although black groupings want radical change – some trying to get it unsuccessfully through radical methods – the government, in the face of conservative opposition, has brought about far-reaching changes and will do so in future.

With preconditions as they are, the best current possibilities for negotiations, in my opinion, are on the local and regional level. I believe that – and here I do not criticise the Joint Management Centre (JMC) system – it is essential to bring in political actors in the JMC's at regional level in the same way as when the Deputy Minister of Police, Roelf Meyer, was made Chairman of the National JMC. A political presence at local and regional level is essential to facilitate negotiation. Security and other officials must operate within a clear political framework spelt out clearly from the top; but at the same time it is also imperative that the real needs and political feelings of people on the ground be fed through to the political decision-makers at the top. This can best be done by politicians.

On the side of the blacks, from the ANC to Inkatha, as Kobus Jordaan intimates, the preconditions are that political prisoners should be released, black political organisations allowed to operate and mobilise freely (meaning that the state of emergency would have to be lifted) and all discriminatory laws abolished. These are stringent conditions bearing in mind that some would be seen by the government as topics for negotiation and that the leverage exercised by the extra-parliamentary and external resistance movements, whether deliberate or in reaction to government action, has been that of civil unrest and disruption. No government would willingly negotiate under conditions of disruption against which it has the capacity to act.

Models

The final major issue was that of constitutional frameworks within which a possible resolution to the conflict could occur. As already intimated there was no unanimity on the utility of discussing constitutional models at what is clearly a very early phase in the movement towards a resolution. All participants in the discussion furthermore agreed that at this juncture modest, piecemeal initiatives were more likely to lead to constructive shifts in positions than any major debate about end-goals.

Nevertheless, some participants pointed out that very broad concepts of what a future settlement could or should be like could assist the early process by possibly providing some reassurance that there was something worthwhile for which to negotiate. In other words, a discussion of frameworks could serve as motivation.

The value of a discussion on goals and models of resolution was underscored by comments made about the nature of the South African conflict. For example, Theo Hanf accepted that the conflict was about more than merely the distribution of incomes, material resources and privilege. If it were simply concerned with quantities or distribution, no particularly complex end-model would be required. As in the case of negotiations over wages and material benefits, the parameters would be clear and the negotiations themselves could begin to demarcate bargaining positions on both sides, which would essentially be about quantities of power and methods of overseeing the distribution of welfare, services, amenities and opportunities in the socio-economic field.

As Hanf pointed out, however, inter-communal conflicts, like that of South Africa, also involved symbols and issues of identity. These are not quantities but are more often than not perceived as absolutes. One cannot divide or redistribute a symbol.

Since the relevance of these perceived symbolic absolutes is so great in the South African debate, it is perhaps necessary for would-be participants in negotiation to be reminded that outcomes can be formulated which will meet emotional and symbolic needs.

The frameworks discussed were the following:

- Unitary democracy with emphasis on individual rights and individual participation in political affairs, with the concomitant goal of maximum equality (called Jacobinism by some participants);

- Devolution or decentralisation of power to smaller units, or in other words, a federalist route;

- A multi-stranded pluralism of interacting group formations within a framework which would allow for informal group mobilisation and bargaining but with the group claims subservient to the needs of the whole. Theo Hanf referred to this model as ideological syncretism (called 'dirty syncretism' by some participants in the debate, but with the word dirty being descriptive of 'creative' untidiness rather than being in any way pejorative);

- Bicommunalism, as outlined in Giliomee's original newspaper article, amounting to a fairly formal mutual acceptance of a partnership in power by a majority-based formation on the one hand and minority-based parties on the other.

As was only to be expected, no agreement was reached on the appropriateness of any one of these models. However, various important and interesting implications of the various options emerged.

The individually-based unitary option was considered by some participants to be unsuited to a non-homogeneous society. 'Jacobinism' in their view could exacerbate internal nationalisms and majority domination was not considered to be any more defensible than minority domination. Hanf made the point that Jacobinism was not an appropriate stance for a non-ruling majority with aspirations to power since it increases resistance to power-sharing in the minority. Jannie Gagiano felt convinced that considerable central State authoritarianism would be necessary to impose an undifferentiated unitary system. Several participants argued that it could mask aspirations to group domination by a majority group in a population.

In regard to the options involving decentralisation or devolution, various participants pointed out that this was not to be confused with current government thinking. The present government programme, as Van Zyl Slabbert and others pointed out, involved a decentralisation of functions rather than of power, which was even more firmly centralised than before. Deputy Minister van der Merwe conceded that the government had been cautious in the early stages but as the process developed a fuller decentralisation of power could occur, conceivably on a regional basis, with the powers developed being substantial and of the same order as the powers enjoyed by homeland governments.

Some discussion centred on the impediments to decentralisation which arise out of regional inequalities in development. Simon Bekker pointed out that certain regions of the country enjoyed a lion's share of resources. Hanf, however, stated that compensating mechanisms could be employed in a federal system, such as the redistribution of government revenue from richer to poorer states, as in the Federal Republic of Germany.

Very little concrete discussion took place on mechanisms for devolving power. Willie Breytenbach believed that the present Regional Services Councils could have their powers extended and that these bodies could evolve into a suitable basis for decentralised government.

Simon Bekker cautioned against being overly optimistic, since some powers were relatively easy to decentralise, such as those dealing with social services, but matters like State security were bound to be dealt with at the centre.

Notwithstanding many promising aspects of decentralisation, some participants felt that it would not meet the requirements of a solution for South Africa. Van Zyl Slabbert questioned the attainability of stability through decentralisation. More generally, participants felt that the goals of the major contenders were so firmly fixed on the prize of central State power that there would be scant commitment to a fragmentation of that power.

Expanding on his paper (see chapter 11), Theo Hanf made a very convincing case for what he termed the 'Indonesian option' of a complex syncretism of group identities within a larger unity. None of the participants could fault the principle in theoretical terms. It was even pointed out that in some respects the group-based structures that had emerged in South Africa could evolve towards a syncretistic unity.

A development and elaboration of existing race-based structures was not what Hanf had in mind, however. A keynote feature of the Indonesian system was that it was based on voluntary association and flowed naturally from commitment within self-determined groups to pursue their own cultural agendas, which were tolerated and absorbed into the wider political interaction in the society.

Regrettably this model could not be discussed more fully. What was, however, hinted at was the fact that a relaxed and mutually affirming interaction of group identities could eventually flow out of a settlement of the current major conflict between a politically solidified minority in power and a majority without participation in central government. However, the stark realities of division of power currently overshadow the cultural and ethnic pluralism that exists in both camps.

The notion of a 'bicommunal' settlement, based on an acceptance of the opposing interests of black and white sub-nationalisms, came in for serious criticism. For some participants it came uncomfortably close to an acceptance of an incompatibility of white and black political interests, or to the legitimacy of a white-oriented mobilisation in opposition to the majority of the South African people. Theo Hanf felt that it would institutionalise and entrench group distinctions even more than is currently the case.

On the other hand, the idea of a bicommunal or dualist resolution is firmly lodged within the reality of South Africa's current conflict. It was argued that at least the proposal for a bicommunal resolution confronted and attempted to deal with the way in which the political conflict had crystallised in South Africa.

Some signs of consensus are emerging but wide differences remain

The issue of the most appropriate model as a facilitator of movement towards negotiation thus remained unresolved, not surprisingly. There was greater concurrence of views on the issue of how group-based interests should be incorporated. The general agreement was that group association should occur on a voluntary basis. Deputy Minister van der Merwe as well as some senior government officials viewed the principle of voluntary group association sympathetically. The majority of the participants were emphatic that enforced or statutory group membership in terms of the Population Registration Act was untenable.

Fanie Cloete mentioned a system applied in New Zealand in terms of which Maoris could choose whether to participate directly in the open system or through a separate ethnic roll allowing the election of minority representatives to reserved seats. Most government spokesmen were of the view that voluntary association could be studied and considered to assess its appropriateness for South Africa in the future.

The central difficulty in the sphere of group mobilisation in politics was the fact that identification with groups is markedly uneven in South Africa. As Theo Hanf pointed out, it is only when all groups have an intimate identification with a political or cultural reference group that they will concede others the right to group solidarity or mobilisation. Hermann Giliomee and others pointed out that traditional Afrikaner in-group identification was weakening, and that the emergence of a more technocratic mode of government might create more flexible perceptions of the way in which groups should be incorporated in the future. Few participants felt, however, that a complete shift to class-based politics as opposed to ethnic mobilisation would occur in the foreseeable future.

The fact that the government intended declaring some residential areas open to all races, as well as instituting non-racial participation in local government for residents in such areas, was seen by some participants as an indication that voluntarism was breaking through. The expectation was that voluntary association would emerge in official policies in the foreseeable future.

This anticipated relaxation of political polarisation did not, however, incline most participants to the view that a general solution was in sight. Simon Jenkins, many participants felt, was uncomfortably blunt when he warned that leaders were always more extreme than their followers and that both sets of political protagonists would act in such a way as to preserve the conflict for some time to come. Given the power realities of the situation, he felt that it was pointless to expect a speedy resolution to the political conflict. Indeed, while he could understand and sympathise with black commitment to the struggle against the government, a confrontation with the present government was strategically unwise, if not futile at this time.

Alternative goals should be adopted which would improve the quality of life and civil rights in what was likely to be a protracted transition period.

Obviously many, if not most participants who were not aligned with government thinking, found Jenkins' views distressing, perhaps even threatening. Nevertheless, if nothing else, these views served to emphasise the size of the challenge in working for conciliation in South Africa, and the need for strategies more creative than those that have failed in the past.

PART III

DISCUSSION AND CONCLUSIONS: PROPOSALS FOR A DEBATE

14

REVIEW: GUIDELINES AND GOALS FOR RESOLUTION

The Editors

It would be exceedingly naive to expect this volume to end with a prediction of an imminent resolution of the impasse in South African politics. In fact, not even the beginnings of a route to such a resolution are sufficiently clear to be generally recognised and agreed upon, and the preceding chapters and discussions confirm this. In broad terms each side expects the other to negotiate as if it had been beaten already in the power struggle. Why is this so? Beneath the recriminations and rhetoric on both sides in the conflict are a few prominent factors which serve to trap the action in what has been referred to, somewhat hopefully perhaps, as a pre-negotiation phase. It is obviously useful to identify these factors as clearly as possible.

IMPEDIMENT ONE: THE RACIAL ADVANTAGE

On the side of the government there is the oft-repeated insistence that white self-determination in regard to 'own' community affairs is non-negotiable. How negotiable it will in fact be when the time for talking arrives cannot be predicted. At this stage one could take the view that it is simply an announcement of a negotiating position, albeit projected as the bottom line, and that it need not discourage participation by the other side. One gains the impression that there is genuine bewilderment in some government circles that blacks are so reluctant to enter into a series of talks.

This bottom line is, however, perceived within a context that imbues it with forbidding undertones. This context is obviously that of the white community having the choice occupations, controlling virtually all management functions, having the lion's share of capital resources, enjoying dominant ownership of territory and housing with, in the latter case, ownership still being protected by formal residential segregation. It is hardly surprising then, that 'self-determination' is interpreted as something akin to continuing control over major resources, infrastructure, territory and amenities. The proclaimed willingness to share power is therefore totally mistrusted. Community self-determination is understood as domination, and if this is to be perpetuated, any negotiation is seen as a farce. The potential benefits of negotiation are anticipated to be marginal; some power may be divided but will hardly be shared.

IMPEDIMENT TWO: WHO CONTROLS THE PROCESS?

The government has moved surprisingly far in creating a framework for negotiation. The proposed National Council will be the forum; it is to have an open agenda; no prescriptions have been made as to topics, rules of negotiation, phasing or methods of taking decisions. Thus the nature of the process itself is open to negotiation, except for one signal factor: the government will still be the controlling power throughout the negotiations, and could stop proceedings, or change the rules at any stage. The only leverage the other participants will have is the power to walk out. The perception, quite understandably, is that the rules seem fair but the dice is loaded.

IMPEDIMENT THREE: MAJOR PARTICIPANTS ARE EXCLUDED

The government approach to negotiation seems to assume that the 'team' on the other side can or should be assembled and mobilised largely from among internal leadership, at best including a non-violent or moderate faction in the expatriate movements.

The fact is, however, that the 'team' on the side of the blacks is manifestly incomplete and, within the constraints of the security system, will remain so. Some major internal leaders could make themselves available, such as Chief Mangosuthu Buthelezi; a number of homeland leaders who are representatives, to a degree, of rural blacks in the national states, and one or two leaders of prominence only in local townships.

Over the years a number of surveys have shown that beyond the leaders mentioned above there is a vacuum without the participation of people currently in prison or exile. The assumption among many if not most politicised blacks seems to be that the government would reject the prospect of negotiating with people whose deep antagonism is borne out by the fact that security action has been taken against them. This is not necessarily the case. Our guess would be that given the prospect of concrete negotiations, the government might find or accept some formula or another to enable, say, individuals from the ANC and certain people currently in prison to participate.

A further problem, however, is that these leaders would have to negotiate without the political 'props' which, in the lack of freedom to mobilise internally, they would need to retain significance as leaders. One prop for the ANC has been the military struggle; a prop for Mandela is the awesome reputation that martyrdom has bestowed on him.

One may argue that scope for internal mobilisation should be allowed, in order to develop a constituency base, during the pre-negotiation phase.

This brings one to the question of the type of mobilisation which an established legal government is likely to allow.

All these problems could conceivably be resolved if other preconditions were favourable and levels of mutual trust improved. Together with the other difficulties, however, the question of who will be on the negotiating team opposing the government, is a forbiddingly complex impediment.

IMPEDIMENT FOUR: THE COSTS OF CONTINUING THE CONFLICT ARE NOT HIGH ENOUGH

The ANC is able to persist with its current programme in the belief that eventual victory and more or less unqualified ascendancy to power is inevitable. Increasingly, world opinion is on its side, external pressures against South Africa have been mounting, the economy of the country is suffering and therefore it might readily appear as if the organisation has everything to gain and little to lose by maintaining confrontation with the government.

The government, on the other hand, can roughly calculate the severe but not crippling economic costs of increasing sanctions and international isolation. It comfortably assumes that, barring an invasion by superpowers, it can ward off any internal uprising or armed incursion and, for the foreseeable future, can maintain its administration and its white support base.

In other words, the costs of the violent stalemate are not sufficiently high on either side to warrant putting their power (or anticipated power on the part of the ANC) at risk in equitable negotiations.

Given these four major impediments, and others which are mentioned elsewhere in the proceedings – see in particular chapter 3 – the pessimism felt by most of the participants at the symposium was understandable. It follows logically that what was termed a bottom-up process, centred on local-level negotiations or regional negotiations, makes considerable sense simply as a means of chipping away at the political log-jam.

Yet, even the slow, incremental process which was debated and recommended by many participants will not necessarily occur. The local-level negotiations which seemed promising all occurred at a time of massive unrest and mobilised community power, both of which have subsided under the impact of the state of emergency. Given that there is no sign of the state of emergency being lifted, the prospects of recovering the earlier momentum of local negotiations are doubtful. The rent boycott in certain townships is perhaps the only action remaining in which community organisations can exercise sufficient leverage to warrant negotiations, but the issue is not sufficiently major to produce negotiations with a general political result. It is unlikely that a different political course will be taken because of a negotiated resolution of a series of rent boycotts; the financial costs involved are minuscule in terms of the national budget.

The KwaZulu-Natal Indaba concerns larger issues – a non-racial settlement in an important region of the country. It is precisely because its implications so meaningfully contradict present government policy that the initiative has been so firmly rejected by the government, as Member of Parliament Johan Steenkamp indicated (see chapter 5).

One can only conclude that unless the effects of the major impediments referred to above can be eliminated or reduced, very little will happen. Not all the impediments are equally important and some will be resolved once others have been removed. For example, should the government become fully committed to negotiate with the whole range of black political leaders, it might release certain political prisoners and allow internal mobilisation (within certain constraints, perhaps). It might even allow a mediating agency, such as a judge, or a specially appointed commission, to take charge of the negotiation process, subject to certain rules which have been established during preliminary negotiations. (This need not exclude participation of the government's own negotiating body, the National Council.)

Two of the impediments mentioned above remain, however. The one, legalised racial discrimination in favour of whites, makes minority rights synonymous with racial privilege, thereby turning an issue which should be negotiable into one which is morally indefensible. The second concerns the perceived costs of full-scale negotiations.

As regards the first issue, it is probably true to say that remaining social apartheid, most particularly the Group Areas laws and segregated government schooling, has to be resolved before the political air will be cleared sufficiently for negotiations to commence on the central issue of power. This is not the place to discuss the issue of residential segregation, but suffice it to say that power-sharing in the context of formal and imposed segregation is impossible, as the conflict between the coloured Labour Party and the government which produced the parliamentary confrontation of late 1988 suggests. If the issue of imposed segregation can be defused then the social costs of a power-sharing settlement will also be substantially reduced for whites.

In the meantime, there is every reason why the major issue of power and political participation should be pursued in the pre-negotiation debate. One method would be to consider ways of raising the costs of not negotiating.

This is essentially one of the objects that the sanctions campaign is intended to achieve. It is, however, subject to some very serious limitations. Firstly, it involves the serious risk that the present government, or conceivably a more conservative successor regime, might opt for a 30 to 40 per cent drop in economic output rather than capitulate to the pressures. South Africa could conceivably continue much as before but as a completely isolated pariah State, with co-opted black conservative partners, grinding poverty suffered mainly by blacks, most white liberals emigrating and with the rest of the world faced with the awful choice between writing the country off or mounting an unbelievably costly military campaign against it, in which it might find itself shooting not whites, but black hireling soldiers.

In order to reduce this danger, the 'sanctions' or pressures to scale down preconditions for negotiations should perhaps be directed at both major protagonists: the government and the ANC. It is precisely because international pressure is perceived by white South Africans as partisan or antagonistic that they offer resistance. Since the pressures on overseas governments to mount sanctions tend to emanate from pro-ANC individuals and organisations, however, an even-handed treatment is probably a very remote possibility.

A more constructive and, ultimately, a more productive course would be to seek to reduce the anticipated political costs of the kind of compromises both the ANC and the South African government would be expected to make in negotiations. As Hanf puts it (chapter 11), the frameworks and objectives must become less incompatible. One way this could occur is by means of a broad constitutional debate on the issues of majority and minority rights, conducted both with the government and with its major protagonists. Constitutional model building at this early stage can, if part of an effective process of communication, hold out possible outcomes of negotiation which both lower the risks of compromise and identify the benefits of settlement. In other words, constitutional models can be employed as motivators.

Potential solutions with unquestionable intrinsic advantages, the models of decentralised power (federalism) and of multiple cultural minorities forming a syncretic unity, are not motivating for South Africa. These are the kinds of systems which may grow out of a resolution of conflict. Both contradict or evade the issue over which the conflict is raging – that of central power institutions. If a model is to be of any use as a precursor to a process of settlement, it must deal with power at the centre.

This does not mean that the decentralised or multiple-identity options should not be pursued vigorously. Whatever the impediments, the search for solutions at the level of city politics or regional politics is one worthwhile course of action. To the extent that even a fragmented system will require some vital centralised power in regard to matters such as national security, supra-regional development strategies, overarching economic policy and the like, the problem of power over central government institutions will remain vital to the outcome.

Unitary solutions have scant potential to motivate the white political establishment. While the ANC, in its most recent review of its policies, appears to be considering various forms of protection of minorities, such as property guarantees and a bill of rights, it does not offer any form of guaranteed *participation* by a party with a white power-base. The unitary, individual-based alternatives require from whites as a group a relinquishing of power – a political capitulation in return for which they as individuals will enjoy protection against discrimination and the right to pursue cultural commitments. It offers too few incentives for self-conscious communities, particularly conservative Afrikaners, for whom control of their own destiny has been a fervent endeavour for many decades.

Seen from the white vantage point, therefore, and by a process of elimination, one arrives at some form of 'partnership' or co-determination model as the obvious compromise. This was termed 'bicommunalism' by Giliomee. For present purposes we might use the more neutral term of co-determination. On the one hand, as pointed out in the previous chapter, it is dangerous in that it could solidify racial antagonisms or, as Theo Hanf put it, institutionalise group differences, in the very process of negotiating a settlement.

Notwithstanding this danger, it has the following advantages:

- It directly touches the essence of the conflict, which is between white minority vested political interests and majority political aspirations.

- It is appropriate to the likely process of resolution in negotiations, in which the major bargaining will probably be between a grouping broadly under the leadership of the white governing party and a grouping broadly or closely aligned with Africanist aspirations. In the conference between the ANC and a group of internal South Africans in Dakar in 1987, it was the ANC delegation that insisted that there should essentially be two sides at the negotiating table. In other words, notwithstanding the fact that there will be other groupings marginal to both the two major protagonists, it will conform perfectly to the basic *realpolitik* of the conflict situation. In this sense it might be much like the settlement of the Union in 1910, where behind all the participants were two major forces: Afrikaner nationalism and British imperialism.

- It also probably correctly anticipates the implications set out in Gagiano's chapter in the sense that as negotiation draws near, there will be a consolidation of white interests around a single ethnic bargaining position.

All this leaves one major question unanswered – what could it offer African nationalists or, alternatively, the ANC? If it is aimed at genuine co-determination it will offer the African nationalists equal status in the running of the country. If it involves constraints on power the constraints will be equal and mutual. This may fall far short of the ideal of liberation under an unconstrained popular leadership, but it can conceivably offer joint 'second prize' as an alternative to a decade or more of armed struggle, exile, the impoverishment of the black masses and possibly the destruction of the major economy on the continent.

Furthermore, it need not be a formula for entrenching polarisation. As a form of 'grand coalition' it could lead progressively to a relaxation of tensions between major protagonists as occurred between the religious groupings in the Netherlands, the politico-religious factions in Austria and as could happen between the ethnic formations in Nigeria.

Put very briefly, it could result, say, in a form of government in which race classification is abolished but with everyone having the choice of either exercising a particular 'communal' franchise or of voting on a common, non-racial roll. Two chambers of parliament might exist: a majority group chamber and a chamber of minorities. Both chambers would have to approve legislation – a form of concurrent decision-making. A cabinet could be drawn from both chambers with roughly equal representation. One chamber, probably the majority chamber, would elect a State President while the other would elect a Prime Minister, as was the case in Lebanon when a form of political accommodation existed there for a period.

One disadvantage normally predicted is that disagreements between two chambers could lead to recurring situations of stalemate or even crises in government. Obviously deadlock-resolving mechanisms, perhaps involving the supreme court, would have to be created. White and other minorities would also fear that the constitution would be usurped by the majority house. For this reason it would perhaps be necessary to aim for a balance of senior personnel in the army.

The details suggested above are less important than the principle. If both the major white political grouping and the resistance movements were to agree in advance, and merely in principle, to some form of equal co-determination solution, even as a transitional arrangement, serious negotiation about a national settlement could become feasible for the first time.

This type of accord would be a variant of what is termed consociation, which has been suggested before and rejected by both sides. The inclination will no doubt be to reject these suggestions as well, simply because they fall short of the major political aspirations involved. One could, however, simply ask what the alternatives might be. The alternatives promoted by both sides are impracticable, as they involve the unrealistic goal of each side requiring of the other to capitulate in terms of present commitments, which neither will entertain, nor is likely to, for many years to come.

We would suggest that the only alternative to co-determination which respects the realities of the situation is a slow, piecemeal process of building up to a solution by pursuing settlement of particular issues or in certain regions or cities. Even this piecemeal process will require some acceptance or encouragement from the major protagonists; encouragement which they will not give unless they can both conceptualise an outcome which promises more gains than losses. Whatever its demerits, which are substantial, there simply may be no realistic alternative to co-determination.

As Giliomee has already mentioned, Robert McNamara (1982) argued that a solution in South Africa should do 'two absolutely essential things: it must assure the blacks full participation in genuine political power. And it must protect the whites against a winner-takes-all form of majority rule'. The Study Commission on US Policy towards Southern Africa in 1981 made the interesting point that the non-negotiables on either side were 'both the core of the problem and, because the non-negotiables are not necessarily irreconcilable, the key to its solution' (1981: XXIV). Lijphart (1985) quotes both sources above and many others in support of the argument that the absence of viable alternatives makes balanced power-sharing or co-determination the most logical political resolution.

We have moved to the conclusion that influential South Africans and concerned actors in the West might profitably attempt to persuade both the South African government and the ANC to consider a bipolar accommodation, or co-determination, as a basis for mutually rewarding compromise in preference to an indefinite struggle. Nothing in the debate contained in this volume was able to convince us that any alternative goal could, within a reasonable time frame, be sufficiently persuasive on both sides of the conflict to be effective in lowering resistance to negotiation.

This might suggest that we have developed a blind faith in a consociational form of resolution; a bi-ethnic mutual accommodation. Far from it — we are more than painfully aware of the many serious limitations of consociationalism as a prescription for South Africa's future. Like Adam and Moodley (1986) we accept that fairly advanced industrialization and a consumer society have introduced great commonalities in South African values across all so-called ethnic groups, and that cultural differences are myths as much as realities. We also accept that the similarities between categories of people will be dramatically increased if formal structures of discrimination are abolished. Furthermore, we know that so-called cultural adherence is an orientation which is true of some whites, and some Africans, and some Indians, but that the majority of the population, in its longer range political orientations, is moved far more by the non-racial ideal of convergence. The idea of co-determination is based quite simply on the reality of a bipolar conflict over central State power. It need not even be defined as culture, class, colonialism or anything else. It is there.

We are not attempting, therefore, to impose some form of ethnic explanation on the society and to move on to a bicultural resolution. Our explanation of the system is more simple, indeed cruder in a sense. Whites, through the remarkably consistent form of social 'closure' called apartheid, have over time been able to establish a life-style which is not necessarily qualitatively different from that of the urban majority, but which is *quantitatively* distinct. South Africa is a Third World society in the middle range of development (and falling behind in relative terms). It therefore has a relative shortage of resources — fiscal resources, welfare budgets, opportunities for well-paid productive employment, developed amenities, social infrastructure and educational opportunities of high quality. In this environment apartheid has in the past fenced in those resources and amenities which the most technically and financially developed segment of the population – the whites – has been able to create with the assistance of political power and black labour. As Schlemmer (1977) has argued, it is not so much culture which makes South Africa a divided society but this 'popular materialism'. It is more comprehensive than the privileges enjoyed by small élites in other greatly unequal societies. It is understood by whites as 'First World standards' which they need to defend. It is not so much culture in the sense of deeply imbued values and rituals, but 'material culture' which has been constructed around power.

We could, therefore, quite easily adopt a far more conventional way of explaining South African society; we could give 'material culture' a simpler and more pejorative description as 'race privilege' and like many — if not most — other analysts, simply call for its removal by persuasion, pressure or protest.

However, we have taken another position because–

- culture of origin and nationalism, while currently obscured by the above-mentioned popular material concerns, is a latent force particularly among Afrikaners and will probably come to the fore under duress;
- the material culture of privilege, sadly but inevitably, is linked intimately with managerial experience, ability to mobilise and deploy capital and entrepreneurial aptitudes which, if dislodged abruptly or constrained severely, will make the entire society poorer;
- above all, the material culture of whites has developed its own mythology and popular commitments which will be defended as viciously as if they were a unique national identity under threat, with all the force which a relatively large and sophisticated security apparatus can bring to bear.

We have therefore suggested the co-determination model as one that might help to persuade both sides in the conflict that a compromise situation which will yield equal, second-best rewards and privileges to both groups of protagonists, will be the most obvious way of promoting their realistic interests. It will most certainly take no longer to achieve meaningful benefits than the present war of attrition which the government and the resistance movements are waging against each other, with international sanctions contributing to the destruction.

Hence our conclusion is no more than strategic and is most certainly not essentially related to any theory of culture or a conceptualisation of the grand benefits of consociationalism. Nor are we boundlessly optimistic. All the major protagonists are very far from achieving success with pressure strategies and mutual destruction. The very different resources and locations of the government and the ANC will also ensure that a collapse of either side is equally unlikely. Simon Jenkins' 'no-solution solution' may be the most valid anticipation of the medium-term future.

Nevertheless, we do not believe that the future should be left only to the risk- and cost-calculating politicians on either side. Their supporters are simultaneously the victims of their calculations. Co-determination condemns no major agenda to the trash-can of politics, and the constituencies of the political protagonists will lose less and benefit more from its implementation than from any other option in the foreseeable future. We suggest it therefore not as an abstract constitutional solution but as a topic for popular debate which could conceivably begin to alter the calculations of the politicians.

REFERENCES

Adam H, & Moodley K, *South Africa without apartheid: dismantling racial domination*, Berkeley: University of California Press, 1986.

Lijphart A, *Power-sharing in South Africa*, Berkeley: Institute of International Studies, 1988.

McNamara R S, 'South Africa: the Middle East of the 1990s', *New York Times*, 24 October 1982.

Schlemmer L. 'Theories of plural society and change in South Africa', *Social Dynamics*, Vol 3, No 1, 1977, pp 3–16.

Report of the Study Commission on US Policy toward Southern Africa, *South Africa: time running out*, Berkeley and Los Angeles: University of California Press, 1981.